THE ORIENT EXPRESS CHINESE COOKBOOK

Iris Friedlander and Marge Lin

A SPECTRUM BOOK

PRENTICE-HALL, INC., Englewood Cliffs, New Jersey 07632

Library of Congress Cataloging in Publication Data

Friedlander, Iris.
  The Orient Express Chinese cookbook.

  (Creative cooking series)   (A Spectrum Book)
  Includes index.
  1. Cookery, Chinese.   I.   Lin, Marge, joint author.
II.   Title.   III.   Series.
TX724.5.C5F665   641.5′951   79-19386
ISBN 0-13-642173-3
ISBN 0-13-642165-2 pbk.

Design and Production by
Susan Alger Walrath
THE BOOK DEPARTMENT
52 Roland Street
Charlestown, Massachusetts 02129

Printed in the United States of America

PRENTICE-HALL INTERNATIONAL, INC., *London*
PRENTICE-HALL OF AUSTRALIA PTY. LIMITED, *Sydney*
PRENTICE-HALL OF CANADA, LTD., *Toronto*
PRENTICE-HALL OF INDIA PRIVATE LIMITED, *New Delhi*
PRENTICE-HALL OF JAPAN, INC., *Tokyo*
PRENTICE-HALL OF SOUTHEAST ASIA PTE. LTD., *Singapore*
WHITEHALL BOOKS LIMITED, *Wellington, New Zealand*

Dedication

To my husband, Richard
I. F.
To my daughter, Susan
M. L.

THE CREATIVE COOKING SERIES

Every recipe in each of our cookbooks has been kitchen tested by the author.

BOOKS IN THE CREATIVE COOKING SERIES

Contents

Acknowledgments *We wish to thank Rebecca Caruba, Madame Grace Zia Chu, Samuel Krasney, Florence Lin, and Elisabeth Lambert Ortiz for their help and encouragement, and Nancy Mellon, who brought the two of us together.*

I. F. and M. L.

About the Authors

My interest in Chinese food began as a child, when I was taken to New York City's Chinatown for Sunday suppers. The little restaurant my family went to, Joy Garden, was one flight up at 48 Mott Street. We usually ordered the same Cantonese menu: *wonton* soup, barbecued spareribs, butterfly shrimp, chicken with almonds, and fried rice. At an early age I learned to eat these dishes with chopsticks. For dessert we had preserved kumquats or mixed fruits in heavy syrup, pineapple chunks, or ice cream. Finally fortune cookies arrived on a little plate. They were eagerly broken open, their printed slips read.

After the meal we walked along Mott and Pell Streets looking at the sights—groceries with unfamiliar vegetables,

Preface

vi

curio shops, fish stores with tanks of live carp, hurrying residents, and other strolling tourists. (Today Chinatowns everywhere still beckon to me. Each summer I visit San Francisco and enjoy exploring Grant Avenue, Stockton Street, and many narrow lanes and alleys in between.)

In later years I continued my early culinary interest professionally, as Picture Editor for Time-Life Books' volume *The Cooking of China.* During that period I worked with Grace Chu, renowned teacher, author, and consultant. At the China Institute of America, in New York City, I studied the basics of Chinese cooking with her. Soon after I took lessons in advanced, gourmet, and banquet Chinese cuisine with the dynamic, delightful Madame Chu in her own fascinating kitchen.

While editing *The Cooking of China* I was fortunate to work with Florence Lin, its principal consultant. Mrs. Lin, a successful author, teaches at the China Institute. I attended her specialized courses in Chinese rice, noodles and dumplings, and Chinese vegetarian cooking. Eventually I began teaching students of my own how to buy, prepare, and eat Chinese ingredients. It was a most rewarding and enlightening experience.

My co-author, Marge Manchu Lin, was born in Manchuria, grew up in Peking, married in Taiwan, and was educated in America. We first met in 1973, just after she had returned from a visit to the People's Republic of China. I had wanted to study Chinese, specifically the Northern dialect, Mandarin, and Marge was suitably qualified. She has a master's degree in linguistics and Asian studies from Seton Hall University in New Jersey, and has taught Chinese at the United Nations International School. Presently she teaches both Chinese and Japanese at the World Trade Institute Language School. Not long after I met Marge, we discovered our other common interests—Chinese food and cooking.

It was a mystery to me how Marge, with her demanding career and three children, could prepare fine Chinese meals so effortlessly. Having been taught to use a *wok,* the Chinese cooking pot, and a cleaver, I was surprised to learn that Marge used neither! Yet her dishes were authentic and delicious. I began to realize that good Chinese cooking can be done with regular Western utensils.

Marge couldn't and didn't want to spend a great deal of time in the kitchen. Instead she employed time-saving, practical shortcuts where possible; she didn't use three ingredients or steps when one would suffice. She knew how to save time, money, and effort in her kitchen. At the same time she preserved her Chinese traditions and adapted them to her new situation in America.

I soon became convinced that not everyone interested in Chinese cooking has to take lessons, master tricky techniques, spend hours cutting up ingredients, buy expensive, exotic foods, or use a *wok* and cleaver. It seemed to me that there was a need for a direct approach—a fresh look at Chinese cooking and a return to basics. Without sacrificing authenticity this aim is exemplified in Marge's *home-style* cooking. We want to share with you her recipes, tips, and secrets, presented here for the first time. They give you an inside look at traditional Chinese cooking brought up to date.

This is how we came to write *The Orient Express Chinese Cookbook.*

Iris Friedlander
1979

Whether you are a beginner or an experienced cook, the *Orient Express Chinese Cookbook* takes you quickly to the authentic world of home-style Chinese cooking for everyday use. Our aim is the practical, time-saving, simple preparation of delicious Chinese meals and snacks. This book is not only for families, but for single people, working couples, parents, young Chinese-Americans and teenagers as well. The more advanced cook will find recipes that are challenging, need a minimum of effort, and are plainly and beautifully presented.

Orient Express home-style cooking is different from what you find in Chinese restaurants—simpler, but no less rewarding. After all, the chef is a professional who spends all day in the kitchen, serving hundreds of people many different dishes. You don't. We therefore concentrate on home-style "cooking-without-the-cook" methods that anyone can do without lessons—braising, stewing, steaming, baking, barbecuing, and pickling.

We combine East and West; we meld the traditional with the contemporary to give our recipes a unique, homespun quality. For example, we tell you how to quick fry foods with a saucepan and slotted spoon rather than stir fry with a *wok,* the round-bottomed Chinese cooking pot. You'll also learn about our "cover-shake-stir" method instead of a tricky, intimidating technique.

Introduction

You will find that we use fewer ingredients and steps. Each recipe recommends utensils regularly used in Western kitchens, such as saucepans, skillets, and slotted spoons; therefore, you do not have to buy any Chinese cooking equipment. We help you budget your time by listing the minutes required for preparation and cooking of each recipe. In addition, times for nonwork steps—marinating, chilling, soaking—have also been carefully tested and listed.

We have included over 100 recipes on cooking with basic ingredients: soy sauce, water, and oil. These recipes illustrate the basic components of a Chinese meal: soups, staples (rice and wheat), and salads. Special added features are chapters on snacks and beverages, with the latest information on imported Chinese wines and spirits. We have also included "tips" after recipes to help insure the success of the dish and to make preparing it easier.

In addition to home cooking, we introduce you to store-to-table products from the Chinese grocery, delicatessen, and bakery. This unique section guides you through these marketplaces to help you supplement your cooking as the Chinese do. For example, we describe some of the things you'll find at the "cooked meat" shop, and recommend ready-to-serve canned, bottled, packaged, refrigerated, and frozen comestibles. We have personally selected urban and suburban stores for you to visit nationwide. The **Orient Express Chinese Shopping List** has 50 items in English and Chinese to help you on your next jaunt. Clip it out and take it with you.

In the **Menus** section you'll get ideas on how to use recipes and bring them together for family-style meals, buffets, outings, tea, and wine parties. You'll also enjoy the suggestions for vegetarian dishes, kids' favorites, and homemade edible gifts.

Take this book with you into the kitchen—don't let it gather dust on a shelf. It will bring you and not just your guests the pleasure of relaxed cooking. We hope the *Orient Express Chinese Cookbook* gives you a new outlook and brings you many rewarding hours of home-style Chinese cooking.

A Note About Chinese Papercuts

The charming illustrations in this book are reproduced from authentic Chinese papercuts. Paper cutting is one of China's oldest, most popular, traditional folk arts.

Two types, scissor-cuts and knife-cuts, originated in North China. They were used to decorate the white paper or glass windows there, and came to be called "window flowers." The women of farm families usually made the red or blue paper cutouts forming silhouettes and pasted them on the windows to add color and lively designs that were visible from both sides. They were especially appreciated during cold, dark winters.

A scissor-cut requires a pair of scissors, a single sheet of solid, brightly colored paper, and a deft hand. Knife-cuts are done with a sharp instrument that will cut through several layers of paper. Typically scissor-cuts depict subjects close to home and heart: children, farming and harvesting, birds, animals, insects, fruits and flowers, and even work-related events or legendary figures.

Ultimately the use of "window flowers" broadened. They began to symbolize joy and happiness at the time of the New Year festival. They appeared as decorations on gifts, lanterns, and food containers. Papercuts were also used for embroidery motifs on pillows, cotton prints, and children's clothes. Today papercuts are made throughout China, with stylistic variations from region to region.

Papercuts selected from the collection of Iris Friedlander

How to Start Cooking

Utensils Make an inventory of your cooking equipment: bowls, knives, pots and pans, measuring cups and spoons.

Determine the capacity of your saucepans and skillets (see **Measure for Measure** in the **Appendix**). Find those utensils that might combine to make a steamer (see p. 48).

Staples Check your kitchen to see which of the following staples you have on hand. Add those you haven't checked on the list below. Also review the *Orient Express* **Chinese Shopping List** at the back of the book.

— all-purpose soy sauce

— Chinese dried mushrooms

— rice

— cornstarch

— oil

— salt

— sugar

— pale dry sherry

— Oriental sesame oil

— tea, green and black

All of these items can be stored in your kitchen cabinet for a long time.

Organization Have your ingredients within reach. Put measuring spoons near salt, sugar, cornstarch, oil, and soy sauce.

Menus Study the **Menus** section in the back of the book to see how to combine recipes for suggested meals, parties, or snacks.

The Orient Express Way

Choose your first Chinese menu from those recipes marked **Good for Beginners.** Do not attempt too much at first. Cook for one other person or your family before you try a large dinner party.

Recipes   Read and study each recipe *twice* before you begin.
Check which ingredients and utensils are required.

Lists   Make a shopping list and check the **Shopping Sources** section in the back of the book for groceries, bakeries, and liquor stores. Try doing your marketing at least one day in advance.

Preparation   Use fresh vegetables and meats as soon as possible for the best taste and nutrition.
Cut and measure all ingredients ahead of time. Place them in bowls and dishes ready to use. Much preparation can be done hours before; check **Tips** at the end of each recipe.

Table   Preheat your oven for baking or keeping foods warm.
Set your table in advance. If you have chopsticks, place a pair to the right or in front of each main bowl or plate. Get out serving platters, bowls, spoons, and ladles.
Relax and enjoy yourself!

Saving Time

Timing   Use a kitchen clock or timer.

Boiling   Bring water or stock to a boil over high heat in a heavy saucepan with the lid on.

Soaking   Use boiling water to soften dried Chinese mushrooms and "cloud ears" (small, crinkly, dried tree fungus).

Cooling   To quickly cool salad ingredients, vegetables, and noodles, plunge them into a bowl of cold water with ice cubes for 10 to 15 minutes.

Cutting Make sure knives are sharp.
If more than one recipe calls for the same ingredient to be sliced or minced (garlic, scallions), do it all at once.
Line up long, slender items for quicker slicing: celery stalks, Chinese sausages, asparagus, scallions, carrots.

Organizing Keep knives, measuring utensils, and garbage disposal container close by so that you don't waste steps in the kitchen.

Measuring Measure salt, sugar, and cornstarch for different recipes at the same time and put on separate pieces of clean paper; check **Measure for Measure** at the back of the book.

Freezing Partially freeze meats and poultry for ½ to 1 hour for quicker slicing; pieces come out looking neater, too.

Quick Frying Shake off any excess water from vegetables for quick frying and drain them up to an hour ahead.

Preparing Garlic Smash individual garlic cloves with the bottom of a heavy bottle or can to loosen the skin and facilitate peeling before crushing or mincing them.

Checking Appendix Check the **Appendix** for the **Time Index** and **Store-to-Table** products. See **Short Notice** suggestions in **Menus**.

Saving Money

Using What You Have on Hand Use regular Western cooking utensils instead of buying Chinese utensils, such as a *wok*, bamboo steamer, or cleaver.

Using Chopsticks These "quick sticks" are rather inexpensive and handy for eating, beating eggs, and cooking. They add a nice Eastern touch to your *Orient Express* meals. We suggest buying them in packages of 10 pairs, rather than 1 pair at a time.

Shopping Purchase imported canned, dried, or bottled Chinese ingredients from a Chinese store, or, if possible, in a Chinatown.

These, as well as Chinese bowls, plates, and tea sets, are likely to be less expensive than if you were to buy them in a department store or midtown shop.

Check your regular grocery and supermarket for fresh Chinese fruits and vegetables before you travel to a Chinatown. Often these items are stocked near where you live and are competitively priced. Also check your stores for sales on staples, meats, and poultry.

Try less expensive animal parts, such as chicken wings, gizzards, drumsticks, and steer oxtails.

Buy whole fresh chickens. Cut and bone the breasts yourself rather than pay the butcher for labor.

Buying Staples   Buy staples in the largest quantities you can store: a 10 or 25-pound bag of rice; 1-gallon can of soy sauce; 5-pound can of hoisin sauce; ½-gallon container of oil.

Buying Tea and Spices   Don't always buy tea in fancy containers; they'll naturally cost more. Buy fancy ones the first time and refill them from plain paper packages or boxes.

Share purchases of tea and spices with friends or neighbors, as these items lose their freshness quickly, and you'll only use a bit at a time.

Buying in Season   Shop for fresh produce in season. Buy winter melon and Chinese cabbage during winter months when they're less expensive; buy snow peas in the warmer months.

Making Stock   Make and use your own pork, duck, and chicken stocks for soups. Save leftover bones, fatty meat scraps from pork chops, spareribs, and chicken carcasses for this purpose.

Gardening   Grow Chinese foods in your own garden (see the **Appendix** for seed sources under **Grow Your Own**).

Checking Menus   Check **Budget Dishes** under **Menus**.

Saving Effort

Using One Pot Use one pot for soy sauce stewing for both cooking and storing the stock.

Marinating Use plastic bags for marinating so you won't have to clean a bowl afterward.

Soaking For vegetarian dishes that may have more than 1 dried ingredient, soak them together. Covering the bowl keeps the flavor in.

Reading Tips See **Tips** at the end of each recipe.

Saving Labels Save labels from canned foods you like so you can find and buy them more readily.

Keeping Canned Foods Keep a supply of canned, bottled, and packaged items on hand, as the Chinese do (see **Store-to-Table: The Chinese Grocery**).

Storing Leftover Ingredients Keep leftover canned bamboo shoots and water chestnuts submerged in water in a plastic container up to 3 weeks; change the water once a week. Because you only use a small amount at a time, you won't waste what you have or need to make extra shopping trips.

Packaged bean curd can be stored, refrigerated, up to 1 week; store fresh bean curd in a container of *salted* water, refrigerated, up to 1 week; change the water every other day or two.

Store fermented black beans, hoisin sauce, and plum sauce in plastic containers in the refrigerator in a separate section reserved for your *Orient Express* ingredients.

Keep oyster sauce and soy sauce in your pantry next to sesame oil and sesame paste—all within easy reach.

Ginger is a snap to store. Simply leave it out in an airy, dry spot. Cut off the brownish scab that hardens and use the moist yellow part. You need not peel it.

Keeping Extra Measuring Utensils
Keeping an extra set of measuring spoons and measuring cups is a shortcut and a worthwhile investment.

Shopping with Our Book
When you go shopping in Chinatown, take *The Orient Express Chinese Cookbook* with you; you'll have the recipes, **Shopping Sources, Shopping List** and handy **Store-to-Table** section to make your marketing quicker and smoother.

Cooking with Soy Sauce

STEWING and BRAISING

STEWING Soy sauce stewing, a unique Chinese "cooking-without-the-cook" method in which foods are briefly boiled, gently simmered, and then steeped, is widely used throughout China. Its basis is a Soy Sauce Stock, called *lu zhi* (thick sauce) in Chinese, composed of wine, water, soy sauce, sugar, and seasonings. This is one of the Chinese cook's favorite home-style methods with many advantages for the beginner in a Western kitchen, as well as the expert who wants to save time and effort.

These are some of the advantages:

1. The ingredients are easy to obtain and can be stored in your kitchen for a very long time.
2. There is a minimum of preparation; one type of food is usually cooked whole and cut up afterward.
3. The same stock, pot, and steps can be used each time.
4. Once in the pot the food doesn't require the cook's constant attention.

Here are the simple steps:

1. Bring the Soy Sauce Stock to a boil.
2. Add the food.
3. Simmer for required time.
4. Steep food in stock.

Cooking with Soy Sauce

The only cooking technique needed is adjusting the flame! And the finished product is versatile. For example, many soy sauce stewed foods can be eaten either hot, at room temperature, or cold. They can be featured as appetizers, snacks, main courses, or sandwich meats. Leftovers can be stored in the stock, refrigerated up to a week, and reheated.

BRAISING A smaller quantity of Soy Sauce Stock and more water is used when braising foods in a tightly closed pot at a low temperature for a long period. This is similar to Western crock pot cookery. It is called "red-cooking" in Chinese because of the color of the food afterward—a brownish red.

Red-cooking can be used for whole or cut meats and vegetables. Usually served hot, these dishes are robust, satisfying one-pot meals that reheat quite well.

Soy Sauce Stock *A master stock of equal parts of water, wine, and soy sauce is a mainstay of the Chinese kitchen. It is used to cook all manner of meat, fowl, eggs, and vegetables. The soy sauce adds a salty flavor that is counterbalanced by a small amount of sugar and the water. The wine neutralizes unpleasant odors and freshens the food.*

With each use the stock has a slightly different personality. Liquid and food mutually enhance and alter each other. Thus, no two families' lu zhi are the same. Often the recipe, and even the stock itself, is passed from generation to generation.

To keep this one-pot master stock recycled indefinitely so it will last for years, follow these steps:

1. Once the stock has cooled, store it covered in your refrigerator. A layer of fat, which acts as a natural seal, will float to the top and congeal into a solid disk to preserve the stock. Remove and discard the fat before each cooking.

2. To keep the stock fresh, either use or boil it once a month.

3. Make at least 3 cups of Soy Sauce Stock, or twice that amount if you have the room. As it decreases, bring it back to a 3 cup minimum by adding equal parts of the liquid ingredients, and don't forget the sugar. Taste the stock before using it to see if it is too salty or not salty enough. Experience will be your guide.

4. If possible, keep one pot just for the stock so you can use it for cooking and storing, thus saving both time and effort.

This master stock is used for all the stewed and braised dishes in this chapter. It can also be ladled over hot plain rice to enliven its taste, used as a dip for Steamed Eggs (p. 50), and added to foods that need more zest.

1 cup all-purpose soy sauce
1 cup Shao Hsing rice wine or pale dry sherry
1 cup water
2 tablespoons sugar

OPTIONAL
2 slices ginger
2 whole star anise
2 cloves garlic
1 scallion

PREPARATION: 1 minute
UTENSIL: 3-quart saucepan with lid
YIELD: 3 cups

STEPS

1. Combine ingredients in saucepan and bring to a boil. The stock is now ready for the food; proceed as specified in each recipe.

TIPS

When cooking food in the stock for the first time, choose a meat or fowl rather than a vegetable or egg dish to get more flavor and fat.

The stock will be enriched if you add any one or all of the following seasonings: pungent ginger, garlic, aromatic star anise, sharp scallions. Remove them after cooking.

Soy Sauce Flank Steak *This lean, smooth-grained cut of beef is favored for Chinese cooking.*

**1 to 1½-pound flank steak, trimmed, 6 inches wide
Soy Sauce Stock to cover**

COOKING: 20 minutes
STEEPING: 20 minutes to overnight
UTENSILS: 3-quart saucepan with lid
long-handled fork

STEPS

1. Bring the stock to a boil. Add flank steak in one piece and bring to boil again.
2. Reduce heat to medium and simmer, covered, for 20 minutes. Turn heat off and steep the steak for at least 20 minutes or as long as overnight. Remove from stock and cut into thin slices. Serve cold or at room temperature.

TIPS

Slice the meat across the grain so it will be more tender.

Flank steak slices are excellent for sandwiches or, arranged in a neatly overlapping circle with spoonfuls of room temperature Soy Sauce Stock ladled on top, as part of a buffet.

PREPARE AHEAD: 8 hours, to 2 or 3 days in stock in the refrigerator.

Soy Sauce Cornish Hen
In China, Cornish game hens are called "baby chickens" and are considered fancy fare that are quite expensive. The "hen" is not always a female. Increasingly, fresh hens are now available.

1 to 1½-pound Cornish game hen, preferably fresh
Soy Sauce Stock to cover

PREPARATION: 2 minutes
COOKING: 20 minutes
STEEPING: 20 minutes
UTENSILS: 3-quart saucepan with lid
slotted spoon

STEPS

1. Bring the stock to a boil. Wash the hen and add to the stock, breast side up. Bring to boil again.
2. Reduce heat to medium and simmer, covered, for 10 minutes. Turn hen over and simmer another 10 minutes. Turn heat off and steep hen in stock, covered, for 20 minutes. Remove hen from the stock; serve hot or at room temperature.

TIPS

Cut the bird in half lengthwise or into 1-inch bite-size pieces, reassembled in the bird's original shape, Chinese style, to be eaten with chopsticks. For color, tuck a sprig of watercress or Chinese parsley under a wing.

PREPARE AHEAD: 2 to 3 days in stock in the refrigerator.

Soy Sauce Chicken Drumsticks

These drumsticks are ideal for buffets, school or office lunches, and picnics.

**1½ to 2 pounds chicken drumsticks
Soy Sauce Stock to cover**

PREPARATION: 5 minutes
COOKING: 15 minutes
STEEPING: 15 minutes
UTENSILS: saucepan with lid
slotted spoon

STEPS

1. Bring the stock to a boil. Wash drumsticks. Cut 2 or 3 diagonal slashes 1 inch long and ¼ inch deep on the fat part of each drumstick. (This makes them cook quickly and evenly.) Add to the stock and bring to boil again.

2. Reduce heat to medium and simmer, covered, for 15 minutes. Turn heat off and steep drumsticks in stock, covered, for at least 15 minutes. Remove from the stock; serve hot or at room temperature.

TIPS

To prepare the drumsticks for outdoor eating, don't slash them. They'll be neater to handle. Simply simmer them an additional 5 minutes.

This recipe can be doubled or tripled.

Soy Sauce "Water Lotus" Eggs

Would you like to try a Chinese way of poaching eggs? Use Soy Sauce Stock, which makes them more flavorful and salty. Done properly, the white and yolk stay intact, evoking the white petals and yellow center of a Chinese water lotus.

4 eggs at room temperature
Soy Sauce Stock to cover

COOKING: 7 minutes
UTENSILS: 2½-quart saucepan with lid
          slotted spoon

STEPS

1. Bring the stock to a boil.
2. Turn heat to low but make sure the stock is still boiling. Quickly and carefully break one egg right over the simmering stock. Wait about 30 seconds or until it firms, then add the second egg; wait, and add the third and fourth eggs, pausing in between. When all the eggs are firm, raise the heat to medium and cook them for 5 minutes or until the yolks are hard.
3. Turn heat off, cover, and leave them until ready to serve hot or at room temperature.

TIP

To make sure the "water lotus" eggs will come out right, break each one into a small bowl and then gently slide it into the simmering stock; or break them into different parts of the saucepan rather than on top of one another.

Soy Sauce Duck
This is the first of three interesting Chinese alternatives to roasting duck. The other methods are steaming and deep frying it.

2 to 3-pound duckling (or half a duck) with giblets, preferably fresh
4 slices ginger
Soy Sauce Stock to cover

PREPARATION: 5 minutes
COOKING: 30 minutes
STEEPING: 20 minutes to overnight
UTENSILS: 3 to 4-quart saucepan with lid
long-handled spoon

STEPS

1. If the duckling is frozen, remove the outer wrapper and thaw it at room temperature for 10 to 12 hours.
2. Add ginger to the stock and bring to a boil.
3. Wash duck and giblets, add to saucepan, and bring to boil again.
4. Reduce heat to medium; cover and simmer for 15 minutes. Turn duck over and cook 15 minutes more. Turn heat off and steep the duck and giblets for at least 20 minutes or as long as overnight. Remove from stock and cut into 2-inch pieces; serve hot or at room temperature.

Soy Sauce Five-Spice Beef
The pleasant aroma of spices will fill your kitchen when you make this dish.

2 to 2½ pounds beef
1 cup Soy Sauce Stock
5 cups water
2 whole star anise
2 tablespoons sugar
1 teaspoon five-spice powder

PREPARATION: 5 minutes
COOKING: 2 hours
STEEPING: 1 hour
UTENSILS: 3-quart saucepan with lid
long-handled fork

STEPS

1. Put all the ingredients in the saucepan, stir, cover, and bring to a boil.

2. Reduce the heat to *medium low*. To keep the liquid from boiling over, leave the lid ajar ½ inch or lay a bamboo chopstick or fork across the outer rim of the saucepan and put the lid on top. Simmer for 1 hour. Turn the beef over and simmer 1 hour more.

3. Turn the heat off and steep beef in stock until it cools (about 1 hour). Cut meat in half, lengthwise, then cut each half across into the thinnest possible slices. Serve cold.

TIPS

The following cuts of beef in one piece are good for the long, slow cooking required here: rump, top or bottom round, eye of round, chuck, beef shank without tendon, and shoulder (or arm).

This meat is excellent for sandwiches.

PREPARE AHEAD: up to 2 weeks in the stock in the refrigerator.

SPICES

Five-spice powder is made of five ground spices: peppercorns, fennel seeds, cloves, cinnamon, and star anise. Look for it in Chinese groceries. As a little goes a long way, this is a perfect purchase to share with friends. Store it in a tightly closed container in your kitchen cabinet. Star anise is called "eight horns" in Chinese because it has eight pointed pods. The English name refers to its starlike shape when whole and its resemblance in smell and flavor to anise seed, which is an acceptable substitute. (Use 1 teaspoon anise seed for 1 whole star anise.) Star anise is reddish brown in color and usually comes in broken pods. Store like five-spice powder. It gives a distinctive aroma to meats and poultry and tea leaf eggs not unlike licorice.

Soy Sauce Meatballs

Soy Sauce Stock to cover

MEATBALL MIXTURE
1 **pound ground beef or pork**
1 **egg, lightly beaten**
2 **scallions, finely sliced**
1 **clove garlic, minced**
½ **tablespoon water**
1 **teaspoon sherry**
¼ **teaspoon salt**

PREPARATION: 15 minutes
COOKING: 10 minutes
STEEPING: 10 minutes
UTENSILS: fork
mixing bowl
3-quart saucepan with lid
slotted spoon
YIELD: 20 meatballs

STEPS

1. With a fork or your fingers, thoroughly combine the ingredients for the meatballs in a mixing bowl. To make each meatball, firmly press, then roll about 1 tablespoon of the mixture into a ball between your palms. Repeat until you use up all the meat (about 20 meatballs).

2. Bring the stock to a boil. Add the meatballs carefully, one at a time, so they hold their shape. Turn heat to medium; cover and simmer for 10 minutes.

3. Turn heat off and steep meatballs in covered stock for 10 minutes. Remove from the stock; serve hot or at room temperature.

TIPS

If you use pork instead of beef, simmer the meatballs an additional 5 minutes to make sure they are thoroughly cooked.

You can keep leftover meatballs up to 1 week in the stock in the refrigerator. Reheat over high heat for 5 minutes.

To make rolling the meatballs easier, wet your fingers with water.

Soy Sauce Pork Spareribs
These spareribs are quick and easy to prepare.

1½ pounds pork or
    beef spareribs
    Soy Sauce Stock to
    cover

OPTIONAL
½ tablespoon
    fermented black
    beans

COOKING: 20 to 25 minutes
STEEPING: 15 minutes
UTENSILS: 3-quart saucepan with lid
          slotted spoon

STEPS

1. Have your butcher cut the ribs apart, lengthwise, then chop them across into 2-inch pieces.
2. Bring the stock to a boil. Add the ribs and fermented black beans. Stir and bring to boil again. Reduce heat to medium; cover and simmer for 20 to 25 minutes until tender.
3. Turn heat off and steep ribs in covered stock for 15 minutes. Remove them along with black beans and serve hot.

TIP

Do not reheat the ribs directly. Instead, bring stock to a boil, turn heat off, and add spareribs, steeping them in the covered stock until they become hot (about 5 minutes).

Soy Sauce Beef Short Ribs
Beef cooked this way is juicy and tender and sometimes separates from the bones. Plain rice soaks up the rich liquid.

2 pounds beef short
    ribs, in 1½ to
    2-inch pieces
    Soy Sauce Stock
    to cover

OPTIONAL
1 whole star anise

COOKING: 1½ hours
UTENSILS: 3 to 4-quart saucepan with lid

STEPS

1. Add the star anise to the stock and bring to a boil. Add ribs and bring to boil again.
2. Reduce heat to *medium low.* To keep the liquid from boiling over, leave the lid ajar ½ inch or lay a bamboo chopstick or fork across the outer rim of the saucepan and put the lid on top. Simmer for 1½ hours. Drain ribs and serve hot.

Soy Sauce Carrots, Peanuts, and Scallions

Even vegetables are transformed by stewing in flavorful Soy Sauce Stock. Peanuts, carrots, and scallions are interesting in combination or prepared singly.

1 cup raw peanuts
2 cups water
4 scallions
4 carrots
Soy Sauce Stock to cover

PREPARATION: 15 minutes
COOKING: 25 minutes
UTENSILS: 2-quart saucepan with lid
slotted spoon
peeler

STEPS

1. Add peanuts to water and bring to a boil. Reduce heat to medium and simmer for 10 minutes. Remove.
2. Trim root ends of scallions and wash. Peel carrots and cut them across into halves.
3. Bring the stock to a boil. Add cooked peanuts, whole scallions, and carrot halves and bring to boil again. Reduce the heat to medium; cover and simmer for 10 minutes. Remove and drain.
4. To serve, mound the peanuts in the center of a plate, put the scallions on top, slice the carrots into 1-inch pieces, and arrange them in a circle around the peanuts. Serve hot or at room temperature.

TIP

Be sure you buy shelled, raw, unsalted, unroasted, skinless peanuts.

Soy Sauce Mushrooms

12 thick-dried Chinese mushrooms
Soy Sauce Stock to cover

SOAKING: 20 minutes
COOKING: 20 minutes
STEEPING: 30 minutes to 2 hours
UTENSILS: 3-quart saucepan with lid

STEPS

1. Soak mushrooms in hot water, covered, for 20 minutes. Cut off and discard stems and leave caps whole.
2. Bring the stock to a boil, add mushrooms, and bring to boil again.
3. Reduce heat to medium and simmer for 20 minutes. Turn heat off and steep mushrooms in covered stock for 30 minutes or 2 hours. Serve hot or at room temperature.

VARIATION

Because dried Chinese mushrooms are expensive, you may want to use 1 pound of fresh mushrooms, 1 to 1½ inches wide. Lightly wash them; trim and discard the tough stems. Cook them for 15 minutes at moderate heat and steep for 15 minutes. Serve hot or at room temperature.

TIP

Try to use dried mushrooms that are 1 to 2 inches wide and ⅜ to ½ inch thick.

Red-Cooked Beef and Carrots

This dish makes a hearty winter stew.

1   cup Soy Sauce
    Stock
2   cups water
1   to 1½ pounds beef
    chuck or stewing
    beef, in 1-inch
    chunks
¾   pound carrots in
    1½-inch pieces

OPTIONAL
1   chunk ginger
1   whole star anise
1   scallion in 2-inch
    pieces

PREPARATION: 10 minutes
   COOKING: 1½ hours
   UTENSILS: saucepan with lid
             peeler

STEPS

1. Bring the stock and water to a boil. Add the beef and seasonings; bring to boil again.
2. Reduce heat to medium; cover and simmer for ½ hour. Taste the meat. If it seems too salty, add ½ cup water and 1 tablespoon sugar. Add carrots and bring to boil again.
3. Reduce heat to *medium low*; cover and cook for 1 hour or until beef is tender. Serve hot.

Red-Cooked Pork and Potatoes

1   pound pork butt, in
    1-inch chunks
1   cup Soy Sauce
    Stock
2   cups water
3   potatoes in 1½-
    inch chunks

PREPARATION: 10 minutes
   COOKING: 1 hour
   UTENSILS: 2-quart saucepan with lid
             peeler

STEPS

1. Combine pork, Soy Sauce Stock, and water in saucepan and bring to boil. Peel potatoes.
2. Reduce heat to medium and cook, covered, for 30 minutes.
3. Add potatoes and bring to boil again over high heat.
4. Reduce heat to medium and cook, covered, for 30 minutes more or until pork is tender. Serve hot.

TIP

Keep peeled potatoes in a bowl covered with cold water until you are ready to use them so they won't discolor.

Red-Cooked Pork Shoulder

When pork shoulder is served with steamed buns in Taiwan, it is called "tiger eating pig" because the buns open to "eat" the pork.

2   to 2½-pound pork shoulder (picnic) with rind, with, or without, bone
3   scallions
⅔ cup Soy Sauce Stock
3   cups water
1   tablespoon sherry

◆

⅔ cup Soy Sauce Stock
⅓ cup water

PREPARATION: 2 minutes
COOKING: 2½ hours
UTENSILS: 3-quart saucepan with lid
long-handled spoon

STEPS

1. Trim root ends of scallions and wash. Put first 5 ingredients in saucepan, cover, and bring to a boil.

2. Reduce heat to *medium low.* To keep liquid from boiling over, leave the lid ajar ½ inch or lay a bamboo chopstick or fork across the outer rim of the saucepan and put the lid on top. Simmer for 1 hour. Add remaining ⅔ cup stock and ⅓ cup water. Turn pork over and simmer for 1 hour more. Turn heat to *low* and cook for final ½ hour.

3. To serve, remove pork from stock, put in center of a platter with scallions arranged on top. Pour 1 cup of the cooking liquid into a gravy boat or pitcher and serve with pork. Serve hot.

TIPS

Red-Cooked Pork Shoulder goes nicely with Steamed Buns (p. 42). Arrange them around the pork and serve at once as they cool off very quickly. Cut off thin slices or chunks of meat and fat, open buns, and stuff them with pork, fat, and a scallion for a succulent miniature "sandwich." You may also serve Boiled Spinach (p. 66); ring it around the meat and ladle sauce over the top. The spinach will absorb the oiliness of the pork.

Rice and Wheat

The first decision a Chinese cook makes before preparing a meal is whether to serve rice or wheat, for these starches are the main courses of the meal rather than the meat, fowl or fish that is customary in the West. Polished rice and refined wheat—white in color, bland in taste, and soft-textured when cooked—go well with all kinds of foods.

Many Westerners think that Chinese food and rice go hand-in-hand. However, rice is a staple grain in the diet of only about two-thirds of the population living south of the Yangtze River. The region's hot climate and plentiful rainfall enable rice to be harvested and cultivated in the rich soils of wet paddies throughout the year.

In South China, rice is often eaten with the three daily meals. The Chinese word *fan,* or "cooked rice," also means "meal." Rice may be eaten as Plain Rice Porridge (p. 29) for breakfast with savory tidbits and pickles, or enriched with egg, ground beef, or chicken for lunch. For at home midday or evening meals rice appears along with soup and other foods. At a banquet this filling fare is served only toward the feast's end, lest any guest should still, by some stretch of the stomach, feel hungry or crave this common grain.

Long- or short-grain rice is delicious by itself—plain, unseasoned, sweet, and natural. Salt and soy sauce are unnecessary. It is important that the rice always be served steaming

Rice and Wheat

hot, for almost nothing is more distasteful to the Chinese palate than cold rice.

Plain boiled or steamed white rice is usually mounded and served in individual rice bowls that can be held comfortably in one's hand. The grains should be moist, tender, and shiny. The bowl is raised to the mouth, and the diner takes alternate bites of rice and the other foods with chopsticks. It is considered impolite, wasteful, even unlucky to leave a single uneaten grain of rice behind. Leftover rice, however, can be fried into a number of delicious combinations using different vegetable oils or animal fats: Fried Rice and Onions in Duck Fat (p. 28) and Vegetable Fried Rice (p. 26) are but two examples.

If the cook decides to select wheat products as the main course of the meal, the choice of menu is much greater. Will it be wheat noodles (*mien*), *wontons,* dumplings, buns, pancakes, or breads? Will these dishes be boiled, baked, steamed, or fried? Sweet or savory? Are the noodles to be mixed or fried; hot or cold? They are mouth-watering considerations.

Because wheat grows in the dry, dusty yellow earth of Northern China's cold, windswept plains and plateaus, it is a basic starch there, just as rice is native to the South. In the past, transportation over China's vast distances was costly and so were food products that were not native to an area. Today, however, one can readily eat fried rice in Peking, capitol of the North, or fried noodles in Canton, heart of the South. But rice is still a Southern specialty and wheat one of the North's staples.

Two Northern specialties, renowned Peking Duck and Pork with Eggs and "Cloud Ears" (p. 104), are traditionally accompanied by crepelike Mandarin pancakes. Steamed wheat buns or breads complement Honeyed Ham, Hunan Style (p. 63), Beef with Onions in Hoisin Sauce (p. 101), Crispy Duck (p. 165), and Barbecued Pork (p. 163) and Chinese Sausages (p. 141). These dishes are warming when snowstorms rage in the north or central provinces.

Plain, hot puffy buns are beloved in North China. We suggest you make them the *Orient Express* way using oven-ready biscuits to save time. Buns with sweet or meat fillings (*see* **Snacks: Sweet or Savory**) are also enjoyed with a meal.

Chinese noodles are available fresh and soft, dried and hard, and with or without eggs in them. Most likely they will have been made the same day in a Chinatown noodle shop. (You need not use the Chinese product but can readily substitute a fine vermicelli or extra thin spaghetti.) These noodles may be flat and wide like *linguine* or thin and round like spaghetti. Or the noodlemakers may cut the noodle dough into small squares for *wonton* skins or larger ones for spring roll wrappers. Little rounds are for dumplings, while larger, 6-inch rounds are for Mandarin pancakes, ready for steaming and filling. *Wonton* skins are especially versatile. They can be filled for soup or snacks or sliced and cooked alone for a hot bowl of Luncheon Noodles, Northern Style (p. 40). They can even be deep fried and dusted with confectioners' sugar for Crispy Twists (p. 138).

We also introduce you to rice noodles, an interesting product made from rice powder in noodle form. They look rather like nylon fishing wire that has become tangled. They will add yet another choice the next time you plan a Chinese meal.

So, think Oriental. Begin by asking yourself, "Rice or wheat?"

Boiled Rice, Country Style

Throughout the South China countryside rice is often prepared by boiling. The cooking water with its vitamins is fed to the family's most important livestock—the pigs. Try this foolproof method of cooking rice; you'll never have to worry about burning it.

1 cup long-grain rice
2 quarts water

COOKING: 15 minutes
UTENSILS: 3-quart saucepan with lid
  colander or strainer
  slotted or wooden spoon
YIELD: 3 cups cooked rice

STEPS

1. Bring water to a boil. Pour rice in slowly; stir a couple of times. Wait for bubbles to come up again and turn heat down a bit. (The rice grains should "dance" in the water as they cook and not stick to the bottom.) Cook for 15 minutes and occasionally skim scum from the top of the water.
2. Drain and serve hot immediately.

TIPS

The only way to spoil this rice is to overcook it; then it loses its tender, firm texture and becomes mushy.

Reheat leftover rice by adding ¼ cup boiling water. Turn the heat to low, cover, and check in 5 minutes. Stir and serve.

Use leftover rice for fried rice dishes. It should never be frozen but can be stored up to 1 week in the refrigerator in a tightly closed container.

New rice is better than old rice that will be drier and require more water. Always wash rice in cold water before cooking to remove any dirt particles and excess starch. Rinsing it until the water runs clear will keep it from becoming too sticky during cooking.

Steamed Short-Grain Rice
This method of preparing rice is trickier than boiling it and requires some practice. The resulting grains stick together more and are moister.

1   cup short-grain rice
1¼ cups water

PREPARATION: 2 minutes
COOKING: 15 minutes
RESTING: 5 minutes
UTENSILS: 1½-quart saucepan with lid
            chopstick

STEPS

1. Wash the rice in cold water until the water runs clear.
2. Add rice and water to saucepan. Smooth rice so it lies flat and is completely covered with water. Cover and bring to a boil (about 4 to 5 minutes).
3. Reduce heat to low and simmer for 10 minutes. Remove from heat and let rest, covered, for 5 minutes. Fluff it with a fork to aerate it. Serve hot.

TIPS

To keep rice from overflowing, you may lay a chopstick across the rim of the saucepan under the lid. If more water is needed during cooking, add 2 tablespoons boiling water at a time.

You can use either Goya, A&P, or River brands of short-grain rice.

Vegetable Fried Rice
A colorful medley of vegetables enhance leftover cooked fried rice. Vegetable Fried Rice is made without soy sauce, rather than Cantonese style with the seasoning liquid. Soy sauce is not necessary and tends to mask the flavor of the grain.

3 cups cooked rice
4 dried Chinese mushrooms
1 carrot, diced
¼ pound fresh, shelled green peas
¼ cup oil
1 teaspoon salt

OPTIONAL
1 square flavored, pressed bean curd in ⅜-inch cubes

SUBSTITUTE
Use frozen instead of fresh peas (1–1½ cups).

PREPARATION: 10 minutes
SOAKING: 20 minutes
COOKING: 7 minutes
UTENSILS: 3-quart saucepan with lid
small bowl
slotted spoon

STEPS

1. Soak mushrooms in hot water, covered, for 20 minutes. Cut off and discard stems and cut caps into ¼-inch squares.
2. Heat saucepan, then oil. Add diced carrots and stir for 2 minutes. Add peas and mushrooms and stir a couple of times; add bean curd cubes, stir, and add salt. Put rice in saucepan and break up clumps as you stir until they are individual grains coated with the oil (about 3 to 4 minutes). Serve hot.

TIPS

Part of the convenience and fun of fried rice is that it can quickly be assembled and made on short notice. Use whatever other vegetables of a firm nature that you may have—lima beans, red or green pepper, onion, sweet corn, or frozen mixed vegetables.

Pressed bean curd squares are flavored with soy sauce, five-spice powder, and other seasonings that vary from shop to shop. Look for them in the refrigerated section of Chinese groceries where they are sold by the piece.

Chinese Sausage Fried Rice

Chinese sausages may be steamed, baked, or fried and used as a delicious sweet complement to rice, eggs, scallions, and red pepper in this dish.

4 cups cooked rice
2 Chinese pork or duck liver sausages
½ cup sweet red bell pepper
2 eggs, lightly beaten
¼ teaspoon salt
2 scallions
¼ cup oil
½ teaspoon salt or 1 tablespoon soy sauce

PREPARATION: 5 minutes
COOKING: 4 minutes
UTENSILS: 3-quart saucepan with lid
slotted spoon
small bowl

STEPS

1. Cut the sausages into ¼-inch slices. Dice the red pepper into ⅜-inch pieces. Slice the scallions into pea-size pieces. Set aside.
2. Heat saucepan, then oil. Add ¼ teaspoon salt to eggs and beat lightly. Pour eggs into pan and stir for 30 seconds or until firm. Add sausage and stir for 1 minute. Then add red pepper and rice; stir constantly until the individual grains are coated with the oil. Add ½ teaspoon salt or 1 tablespoon soy sauce. Mix and stir to bring rice up from the bottom of the pan to the top (about 2 to 3 minutes).
3. Add scallions and stir. Serve hot.

VARIATION

Use ½ cup diced Barbecued Pork (p. 163) in place of the Chinese sausages.

TIPS

Shiny Chinese sausages are made from a mixture of lean and fat pork (sometimes with duck liver added, which makes them a dark brown) and seasonings. The sausages range from 5 to 7 inches long by ¾ inch. They are available in Chinese markets and butcher shops. You often see them hanging in pairs from looped strings or in 1-pound packages of 20 to 24 sausages. To store, wrap sausages in plastic or aluminum foil and keep them up to 1 month in the coldest part of your refrigerator or up to 6 months in your freezer. They defrost quickly. It's a good idea to keep a supply of this useful ingredient on hand.

Fried Rice and Onions in Duck Fat

Duck fat gives the rice, onions, and eggs in this dish a subtle aroma and rich home-style flavor that is indescribably delicious.

1　small onion
¼　cup duck fat
3　eggs, well beaten
¼　teaspoon salt
2　tablespoons duck fat
3　to 4 cups cooked rice
1　teaspoon salt or to taste

SUBSTITUTE
Instead of duck fat use chicken fat or lard. Use 1 cup finely sliced scallions or Chinese leeks instead of the onions.

PREPARATION: 3 minutes
COOKING: 7 minutes
UTENSILS: small bowl
　　　　　3-quart saucepan
　　　　　long-handled spoon

STEPS

1. Cut onions into ½ × ⅜-inch pieces.
2. Add ¼ cup fat to saucepan. Cook over medium heat for 1 minute. Watch fat to make sure it doesn't burn or smoke. Add eggs and ¼ teaspoon salt. Stir in a circular motion for 2 minutes or until the eggs are firm. Remove and set aside.
3. Add the remaining 2 tablespoons of fat, let it melt, then add onions and stir for 30 seconds. Add rice; break it up until the grains are separated and coated with fat. Stir until the rice is shiny and well heated (about 2 to 3 minutes).
4. Add eggs and mix. Add 1 teaspoon salt and stir for 1 minute. Serve hot.

TIPS

For fried rice you can use cold, room temperature, or warm plain boiled or steamed cooked rice. Cooked long-grain rice is best; be sure to break it into clumps and fluff it a bit before frying so the grains will come out separate and whole.

Rice can be fried in vegetable oil, duck or chicken fat, lard, or drippings from Chinese sausages. Each imparts a different flavor, with animal fats yielding the strongest taste.

A big bowl of fried rice can be a hearty one-dish meal.

Plain Rice Porridge *Chinese families like to start their mornings with a bowl of steaming rice porridge—rice that has been cooked in a lot of water until it reaches a somewhat soupy consistency. The bland, soft rice is often accompanied by four or more light, handy side dishes from a can, jar, or soy sauce stock pot. If you've always wondered what's eaten for breakfast in China, here is one menu.*

**1 cup short-grain rice
2 quarts water**

COOKING: 30 minutes
RESTING: 20 minutes
UTENSILS: 3-quart saucepan with lid

SIDE DISHES:
preserved cucumbers
(canned)
dry roasted peanuts
Mixed Pickled Vegetables,
Szechuan Style (p. 87)
pickled Chinese turnips
Deep-Fried Salted Peanuts
(p. 144)

Soy Sauce Eggs (p. 9)
Sugared Walnuts (p. 139)
Salted Broccoli Stems
(p. 83)
Soy Sauce Chicken Wings
(p. 159)
preserved tea melons
(canned)

STEPS
1. Add rice and water to saucepan, cover, and bring to a boil.
2. Turn heat to *very low*. Cook, covered, for 30 minutes. Turn heat off. Let rice rest, covered, for 20 minutes.
3. Serve hot in individual bowls with four of your favorite side dishes.

TIPS
Rice porridge is a basic dish with variations. In South China it is commonly served with salted fish or salted duck eggs.

This dish is particularly easy to digest and is good for infants, older persons, or someone who is sick.

Rice Porridge and Eggs

½ cup short-grain rice
6   cups water
2   eggs, well beaten
2   teaspoons soy
    sauce
2   teaspoons salt
    sesame oil

OPTIONAL
1   scallion, finely
    sliced
    ground pepper

PREPARATION: 3 minutes
   COOKING: 30 minutes
   RESTING: 20 minutes
  UTENSILS: 3-quart saucepan with lid
            small bowl
            chopsticks or fork
            ladle

STEPS

1. Add rice and water to saucepan, cover, and bring to a boil.
2. Turn heat to *very low*. Cook, covered, for 30 minutes.
Turn heat off. Let rice rest, covered, for 20 minutes.
3. Combine eggs with soy sauce and salt. Pour into individual
serving bowls. Bring rice mixture to boil again. Ladle about 1
to 1¼ cups of piping hot rice into each bowl and immediately
beat with chopsticks or a fork for about 1 minute until the
eggs are firm. Serve hot, topped with a couple of drops of
sesame oil and about 1 teaspoon of scallions per bowl.

TIPS

If the rice overflows as it cooks, place one chopstick flat
across the pan to allow steam to escape between it and the
lid.

Leftover rice can be made into porridge; add water, bring
to a boil, and follow recipes.

This soothing porridge is an interesting switch from hot
cereals and can be seasoned to your taste. It is nourishing in
that it provides starch, protein, and iron.

Rice Porridge with Ground Beef or Chicken *This hearty version of rice porridge makes a fine luncheon dish.*

½ cup short-grain rice or ¼ cup short-grain rice plus ¼ cup glutinous rice
7 cups water
½ cup raw chicken breast, cut in 1 × ⅛-inch pieces, or ¼ pound ground beef
2 tablespoons scallions, finely shredded
½ tablespoon sherry
¼ teaspoon salt

OPTIONAL
¼ cup fresh or canned mushrooms, finely sliced
1 tablespoon Szechuan mustard pickle, minced
1 slice ginger, shredded

PREPARATION: 10 minutes
COOKING: 30 minutes
HEATING: 5 to 10 minutes
UTENSILS: 3-quart saucepan with lid
1½ to 2-quart heatproof bowl

STEPS

1. Combine rice and water in saucepan and bring to a boil.
2. Turn heat to *very low.* Cook, covered, for 30 minutes.
3. In a deep bowl put the chicken or beef, scallions, sherry, salt, and one optional ingredient. Pour hot rice porridge on top. Stir gently, cover, and leave 5 to 10 minutes until meat or fowl is cooked through. Serve hot in individual, small bowls.

TIP

Glutinous rice is also called "sweet rice" or "sticky rice." It is a short, plump grain with a shiny, pearllike gleam. After cooking it becomes sticky, but not sweet, although it is frequently used for dessertlike snacks (see December 8 Festival Rice, p. 135). Look for it in Oriental markets.

Fried Rice Noodles with Pork

The noodles used in this fried dish are made of rice powder and water and are sometimes labeled "Rice Sticks" or "Rice Vermicelli." They are quite different in texture from Western noodles.

½ pound rice noodles
½ pound pork loin
¼ cup oil
1 tablespoon garlic, minced
¼ pound fresh string beans
1 medium onion

MARINADE
1 tablespoon sherry
¼ teaspoon salt

SAUCE
½ cup oyster sauce
¼ cup water

SUBSTITUTE
You can replace the fresh beans with 1 cup frozen, julienne-style string beans, but they won't be crunchy.

PREPARATION: 30 minutes
SOAKING: 20 minutes
MARINATING: 10 minutes
COOKING: 10 minutes
UTENSILS: 2-quart bowl
colander
skillet, 9 × 3 inches
chopsticks

STEPS

1. Put rice noodles in bowl, cover with *warm* water, and soak for 20 minutes until they soften and become opaque. Drain.
2. Cut pork into 1½ × ⅜ × ¼-inch pieces. Mix with marinade ingredients and marinate for 10 minutes.
3. Snap off the ends of the beans. Wash and drain well. Cut them into 1½ × ¼-inch pieces. Cut the onion into similar-sized pieces.
4. Heat skillet, then oil. Add garlic, string beans, and onion; mix well. Add pork. Stir and mix for 5 minutes until pork loses any trace of pink and turns brown.
5. Add rice noodles and use chopsticks to thoroughly mix noodles and vegetables.
6. Add oyster sauce and water; stir and mix well, cooking about 3 minutes. Serve hot.

Noodles with Meat Sauce

This is a warming winter dish that originated in North China.

PREPARATION: 10 minutes
COOKING: 10 minutes

1   pound fresh or 1
    cup canned bean
    sprouts
1   pound fresh
    Chinese egg
    noodles, ¼ inch
    wide
1   tablespoon oil
1   cucumber

SAUCE
2   tablespoons oil
2   cloves garlic,
    minced
¾   cup hoisin sauce
½   pound ground lean
    beef or pork
4   scallions, finely
    sliced

SUBSTITUTE
**Instead of Chinese
egg noodles use
No. 10 extra thin
spaghetti and
follow cooking
instructions on box.**

UTENSILS: 3 or 4-quart saucepan with lid
            bowl
            colander
            1-quart saucepan
            peeler
            long-handled spoon

STEPS

1. Bring 3 quarts of water to a boil. Put fresh bean sprouts in a bowl and cover with about 2 cups of boiling water. Leave for 1 to 2 minutes. Drain and rinse under cold running water or chill in refrigerator for 10 minutes until cool.

2. Separate fresh noodles with your fingers before cooking. Add to the remaining boiling water. Cook for 5 or 6 minutes until they are completely shiny. Drain and rinse in cold water to remove excess starch and to keep them from sticking together. Mix with 1 tablespoon oil.

3. While the noodles are cooking, peel and shred the cucumber (see **Tips**).

4. To prepare the sauce, heat 2 tablespoons oil. Add garlic and mix. Add hoisin sauce and meat; mix and stir until the meat turns brown (about 3 minutes). Add scallions and mix.

5. To serve, put the meat sauce, bean sprouts, and cucumber shreds in separate bowls around a big bowl of noodles. The diner adds vegetables to the noodles, selects spoonfuls of sauce, then mixes everything together. Mmmm. Delicious.

TIPS

The noodles can be prepared ahead and left at cool room temperature.

If you use pork, cook it 5 minutes to be sure it is done; but don't overcook the beef or it will be tough.

An *Orient Express* way to shred a cucumber: After it is peeled, start slicing off long pieces, lengthwise, ¼ inch thin, until you reach the seeds. Now turn the cucumber over and do the same on the other side until only the seed core is left. Discard it and cut the cucumber slices into 2 × ¼-inch shreds.

Cold Noodles with Sesame Paste

This dish looks like a veritable vegetable garden—it's a summertime treat in North China. If you like the taste of peanut butter, which sesame paste closely resembles, you're sure to enjoy these noodles.

½ pound dried or fresh Chinese egg noodles, ¼ inch wide
2 tablespoons oil
¼ teaspoon salt

GARNISHES
½ pound fresh or canned bean sprouts
1 cucumber
½ cup red bell pepper or carrots, shredded
2 scallions, shredded

OPTIONAL
1 cup cold cooked chicken breast, shredded (see **Step 3, Celery Salad,** p. 78).

DRESSING
¼ cup sesame paste or smooth peanut butter
2 tablespoons soy sauce
2 tablespoons sesame oil
⅓ cup warm water
½ tablespoon distilled white vinegar
2 cloves garlic, minced

OPTIONAL
1 teaspoon cayenne pepper
½ teaspoon sugar

SUBSTITUTE
Instead of Chinese egg noodles, use No. 10 extra thin spaghetti and follow cooking instructions on box.

PREPARATION: 25 minutes
CHILLING: 10 minutes
COOKING: 10 minutes
UTENSILS: 3 or 4-quart saucepan with lid
bowls
colander
peeler
spoon

STEPS

1. Bring 3 quarts of water to a boil. Put fresh bean sprouts in a bowl and cover with about 2 cups of boiling water. Leave for 1 to 2 minutes. Drain and rinse under cold running water or chill in refrigerator for 10 minutes until cool.
2. Separate fresh noodles with your fingers before cooking. Add them to the remaining boiling water. Cook for 5 to 6 minutes until they are completely shiny. Drain and rinse them in cold water, mix with oil and salt, and put in refrigerator to chill for 10 minutes. These steps can be done hours ahead.
3. While the noodles are cooking, mix the dressing ingredients by combining the liquids and paste and pressing them with the back of a spoon against a bowl until a smooth consistency is reached. Add the garlic and, if used, the cayenne pepper and sugar. Mix again.
4. Shred cucumbers (see **Tips, Noodles with Meat Sauce,** p. 32). Shred carrots (see **Tips, "Cellophane" Noodle Salad,** p. 78).
5. Assemble garnishes in separate bowls surrounding a large bowl of noodles. To eat, each diner places some noodles on a plate, sprinkles cucumber, bean sprouts, pepper or carrot shreds, and scallions on top, adds sesame paste dressing, and mixes everything together. Serve chilled.

Vegetarian Noodles

The textures of four interesting Chinese ingredients—bean sprouts, bamboo shoots, "cloud ear" fungi, and dried mushrooms—add to the special quality of this noodle plate.

12   "cloud ears" (about ¼ cup)
6   dried Chinese mushrooms
½   pound fresh Chinese noodles, ¼ inch wide
2   tablespoons oil
1   tablespoon soy sauce
½   pound fresh or 1 cup canned bean sprouts
½   cup bamboo shoots, shredded
2   carrots, shredded
¼   cup oil
1   teaspoon salt

OPTIONAL
¼   cup water chestnuts, in ¼-inch shreds

SUBSTITUTE
Instead of Chinese noodles use rice noodles or No. 10 extra thin spaghetti and follow cooking instructions on box.

PREPARATION: 25 minutes
SOAKING: 20 minutes
COOKING: 5 minutes
UTENSILS: 3 or 4-quart saucepan with lid
heatproof bowl
bowl
colander
skillet, 10 inches
chopsticks

STEPS

1. Soak "cloud ears" and dried mushrooms in hot water, covered, for 20 minutes. Drain. Cut off and discard mushroom stems. Cut caps and "cloud ears" into ¼-inch shreds.

2. Bring 3 quarts of water to a boil. Put fresh bean sprouts in a bowl and cover with about 2 cups of boiling water. Leave for 1 to 2 minutes. Drain and rinse under cold running water or chill in refrigerator for 10 minutes until cool. (Canned bean sprouts need only be rinsed briefly with the boiling water before being cooled.)

3. Separate fresh noodles with your fingers before cooking so they don't stick together; then add them to the remaining boiling water. Cook for 5 to 6 minutes until they are completely shiny. Drain and put in bowl. Mix gently with 2 tablespoons oil and 1 tablespoon soy sauce for 1 minute until they are well seasoned.

4. Heat ¼ cup oil in skillet over medium-high heat for 1 minute. Add softer vegetables first: bean sprouts and carrots; add firmer ingredients next: bamboo shoots, "cloud ears," and dried mushrooms. Stir until they are completely mixed

(about 2 minutes). Use chopsticks to push noodles and vegetables gently around the skillet. Serve hot.

Tips

Prepare the vegetables hours ahead and leave them at cool room temperature.

Mixing the noodles with oil keeps them from sticking together and makes them shiny.

For an easy way to shred carrots see **Tips, "Cellophane" Noodle Salad** (p. 78).

"Instant" Noodles

Instant, dried, precooked noodles are imported from Taiwan, Hong Kong, and Japan. They come with a dry soup base. Only boiling water has to be added. These coiled and curled noodles have various names: "picnic" noodles, "tourist" noodles, and even "Chinese-style alimentary paste," a name derived from the Italian term for pasta— "paste alimentari." According to U.S. government standards, a product must contain eggs to be called noodles. "Instant" noodles are made from rice or wheat flour, oil, salt, and water—no eggs. But they are still noodles! Look for them in both Oriental and Western markets.

PREPARATION: 2 minutes
COOKING: 5 minutes
UTENSILS: 2-quart saucepan
long-handled spoon

2 **3-ounce packages of "instant" noodles**
1 quart water

OPTIONAL
1 **cup vegetables, in ½-inch pieces:** *bok choy,* **Chinese cabbage (Napa), French-cut string beans, spinach, watercress, bean sprouts, celery**
¼ cup leftover cooked meat or poultry, shredded or sliced into ½-inch pieces: chicken, duck, ham, roast pork

STEPS

1. Bring water to a boil. Follow directions on the package or drop noodles into boiling water.
2. Add one vegetable and/or leftover meat or poultry and bring to boil again. Stir and separate noodles. Add soup base flavorings; cook over high heat for 2 minutes. Stir and serve hot.

VARIATION

Try enhancing the noodles with eggs. After you add the noodles, turn heat to low, but make sure the water is still boiling. Quickly and carefully break one egg right over the simmering liquid. Wait about 30 seconds or until it firms; then add a second egg. Wait until it firms, raise the heat to medium, and cook for 5 minutes. Stir in ¼ cup finely sliced scallions and serve hot.

TIPS

Celery and watercress do not need to be cooked. Put them in the bottom of the bowls or into the pot last.

"Instant" noodles are especially handy for outings. To prepare them before you leave home, put them into a wide-mouthed thermos bottle that has been prewarmed with hot water. Add the leftovers, soup base, and last, the boiling water. Cap tightly. Omit the vegetables; they'll get yellow and soggy.

For a heartier noodle dish, add only half the water specified for soup.

Wontons

Wontons appear as snacks and in wonton "soup"—so called because the wontons are served in broth. They require practice to perfect, but once perfected, will impress any diner.

40 *wonton* **skins (about ½ pound)**

FILLING
½ pound ground beef
1 tablespoon water
½ tablespoon sherry
½ teaspoon salt
¼ teaspoon sesame oil

SUBSTITUTE
Instead of all beef use ¼ pound ground beef and ¼ pound ground pork, or all pork, no water, and ¼ teaspoon ginger, minced.

PREPARATION: 30 minutes
UTENSILS: mixing bowl
fork
YIELD: 40 *wontons*

STEPS

1. In a mixing bowl thoroughly combine the filling ingredients with a fork or your fingers.
2. With the *nonfloury side up* put a *wonton* skin in the palm of your hand. Put a teaspoon of the filling in its center. Fold it over the filling to form a triangle. Press all around the filling with your thumbs so the *wonton* won't open during cooking.
3. Dip your finger into water and moisten one of the long ends of the triangle. Bring both ends together and overlap them; press at the moistened spot to form a little "nurse's cap." This is your finished *wonton*. Repeat until you have used up all the filling.

TIPS

It is best to use *wontons* immediately for *Wonton* "Soup" (p. 39) or Deep-Fried *Wontons* (p. 143). If you have made extras that you don't want to use right away, place them carefully in a pie pan so they are slightly separated from one another; cover tightly with aluminum foil and freeze up to 1 week. To cook, do not defrost them; just add a little extra boiling or frying time.

Frozen *wonton* skins will be drier than freshly bought ones. When thawed, cover them with a clean, moist towel.

Care should be taken even with fresh *wonton* skins to keep them from drying out; they should be soft and supple to handle. Take only a dozen at a time from the package and keep the rest wrapped in wax paper or plastic covering.

Each *wonton* skin has one side with more flour on it than the other. The flour keeps the skins from sticking to one another in the package. If you have the floury side up to receive the filling, the dough won't stick when you press around the filling and the *wonton* will open during cooking.

Wonton "Soup"

In China wontons were traditionally served as a snack, not a soup. Fifteen or more wontons per diner, less if served in broth, would make a main luncheon course. They would be especially welcomed as a midnight snack after a game of mahjong.

30 *wontons* (p. 38)
 2 cups chicken stock
 2 cups water
 1 pound fresh spinach
    or 1 cup watercress
    salt
    sesame oil

SUBSTITUTE
For fresh spinach substitute a 10-ounce package, cut in half, of frozen spinach or any leafy green that can be cooked.

PREPARATION: 5 minutes
  COOKING: 10 minutes
  UTENSILS: 3-quart saucepan with lid
        colander

STEPS

1. Bring stock and water to a boil. Add *wontons* and bring to a boil again.
2. Wash spinach or watercress well and drain. Cut leaves and stems in half. Add greens to soup and bring to boil for a third time.
3. Season with salt to taste and dribble sesame oil on top. Serve hot.

TIPS

In China the pink ends of the spinach stems are believed to contain the most iron—and, incidentally, add a touch of pastel color—so they are used.

For a main luncheon course add 1 cup of shredded Chinese cabbage (or any other leafy vegetable that can be boiled) and ½ cup cooked, shredded Barbecued Pork (p. 163).

To serve as "soup," give each person 4 to 6 *wontons* and divide the broth accordingly.

Luncheon Noodles, Northern Style

Wonton skins are transformed into noodles with a knife. These slippery slices mingle with crunchy bits of Szechuan mustard pickle and scallion rings in a light, silky broth.

2 cups chicken stock
2 cups water
20 *wonton* skins (about ¼ pound)
2 scallions, finely sliced
salt to taste
1 teaspoon sesame oil

OPTIONAL
1 tablespoon Szechuan mustard pickle, minced
flour

PREPARATION: 10 minutes
COOKING: 10 minutes
UTENSILS: 3-quart saucepan with lid
slotted spoon

STEPS

1. Combine chicken stock and water in saucepan. Add Szechuan mustard pickle. Bring to a boil.

2. Cut the *wonton* skins into three strips about 1 inch wide. To prevent them from sticking together during cooking, spread them out like the spokes of a fan or dust them with a little flour. Toss them gently with your fingers to shake off any excess flour.

3. Reduce heat to medium. Sprinkle a handful of noodles at a time into the pan and stir constantly to keep them separated. After all the noodles are in, continue to stir for 2 minutes or until they change color and look shiny and translucent. Cook and stir 1 minute more. Add the scallions and stir. Pour noodles into a large bowl and dribble sesame oil on top. Salt to taste. Serve hot.

VARIATION

Add ¼ or ½ cup of either shredded *bok choy*, Chinese cabbage (Napa), or spinach after the stock comes to a boil. Stir; add noodles. For a last-minute garnish, add ½ cup cooked, shredded ham or barbecued pork.

Sweet Noodles

The idea of sweet noodles may be new to you, but we have a hunch they'll be very popular, especially with youngsters. Chinese families serve them as a light luncheon dish or bring them out after an evening of mahjong as a cue to the players to leave—but not without full stomachs. Try them at your next card party.

**2 quarts water
20 *wonton* skins (about ¼ pound)
2 to 3 tablespoons sugar
sesame oil**

PREPARATION: 2 minutes
COOKING: 7 to 8 minutes
UTENSILS: 3-quart saucepan with lid
slotted spoon

STEPS

1. Bring water to a boil. Cut the *wonton* skins into 4 strips about ¾ inch wide. Separate the strips (see **Step 2,** Luncheon Noodles, Northern Style, p. 40).

2. Reduce heat to medium. Take a handful at a time, sprinkle the noodles into the saucepan, and stir constantly to keep them separated. After all the noodles are in, continue to stir for 2 minutes more or until they change color and look shiny and translucent.

3. Put noodles in individual bowls and cover them with water from the pan. Season to taste with sugar and a drop of sesame oil. Serve hot.

Steamed Buns
Steamed buns are very popular in North China, because wheat, not rice, is the main staple. Traditionally, buns were steamed at home rather than baked, for Chinese kitchens were not equipped with ovens.

**10 plain oven-ready refrigerated biscuits
1 tablespoon oil**

PREPARATION: 10 minutes
STEAMING: 10 minutes
UTENSILS: steamer
wax paper
spoon
fork
heatproof plate
YIELD: 10 buns

STEPS

1. Prepare a steamer (See p. 48).
2. Cut wax paper into 10 squares of 2 inches each.
3. Separate the biscuits and press each one flat with your palm to a diameter of 2 inches. Brush a little oil on top of each circle with the back of a spoon and fold it over to form a half-moon; make sure the oiled sides touch each other.
4. Use the side of the tines of a fork and press 3 or 4 equidistant indentations into the rounded edges of the dough. Or you can follow the curve of the bun and use the flat tines to press indentations on the edges of the dough. These indentations help keep the bun closed during steaming. Place each bun on a wax paper square.
5. Put the buns on a plate in the steamer and bring water to a boil. Reduce heat to medium and steam buns, covered, for 10 minutes until they puff up and become shiny. Serve hot immediately as they cool quickly.

Lift finished buns carefully as they will be quite hot.

Steamed buns are excellent for absorbing the juices of Red-Cooked Pork Shoulder (p. 17), Honeyed Ham, Hunan Style (p. 63), Flank Steak with Onions in Hoisin Sauce (p. 101), Steamed Chinese Sausage (p. 141), Crispy Duck (p. 165), and Barbecued Pork (p. 163).

Cooking
with Water

STEAMING and BOILING

STEAMING Steaming is one of the oldest known cooking methods in China. Even now it continues to be a standby of the Chinese chef, whose kitchen is equipped to steam foods of all kinds. Steaming has many pluses:

1. It is another "cooking-without-the-cook" method.
2. It is economical; 2 or 3 dishes can be steamed together.
3. Foods cook in their own juices and retain their natural flavors and vitamins.
4. Steamed foods are easily digestible.
5. Before steaming, all the seasonings are added at once.
6. Food is often steamed and served in the same plate or bowl.
7. Steaming is a good way of reheating rice, meat, poultry, and fish.

Although the method of steaming is the same in both East and West, the ingredients and type of steamer differ in China. In a Chinese kitchen, which rarely boasts an oven, eggs, potatoes, crabs, duck, chicken, pork, bean curd, sausages, buns, dumplings, fish, and breads are steamed.

Cooking with Water

Utensils A traditional Chinese steamer is made of handwoven bamboo, while the Western steamer is usually made of tiers of aluminum. However, you don't have to buy either version. For home-style cooking the *Orient Express* way, you can assemble a one-level steamer by using cooking utensils already on hand. You need 3 basic utensils:

1. ***A pan with a tight-fitting lid:*** a saucepan, roasting pan, skillet, casserole, or electric frying pan. The pan should be deep and wide with the lid curved or domed to allow steam to circulate freely.
2. ***A support for the food container:*** a cake-cooling rack, roasting pan rack, open-ended tin can, pair of chopsticks, 2 pieces of wood, or inverted bowl.
3. ***A heatproof food container:*** a plate or bowl. It can be round or oval, shallow or deep.

When assembling a steamer, it is important to allow enough space for your fingers with pot holders or towel to lift out the food container, which will be very hot after steaming. A round bowl or plate in an oval pot, or vice versa, makes it easier. Or you may want to buy an inexpensive, imported, three-pronged aluminum hot-dish retriever sold in Chinese hardware stores.

Water How much water should you use to steam foods? Always have at least 1 inch of hot or cold water in the bottom of the pan. The water should be below the level of the food container. Of course, the amount of water will vary depending on the food, the size of your pan and food container, and the steaming time. If the steaming time is only 5 or 10 minutes, you won't have to check the water level. If the steaming time is longer, check the level and add *boiling* water if necessary. (It's a good idea to have a kettle of boiling water on hand when steaming foods for a long period.) With experience, you will eventually learn to judge the proper water level.

When lifting the lid of the steamer, be sure to tilt it *vertically away from your face and hands*. A blast of hot, live steam, which is the same temperature as boiling water, can burn! Also avoid dripping water from the inside of the lid onto the food.

Method To steam, follow these steps:

1. Add water to the pan.
2. Put the support in the pan and place the food in the container on top of the support. Make sure the container is level and steady.
3. Turn heat on and bring water to a brisk boil. Cover the pan. Reduce heat to medium.

Adding the food *before* bringing the water to a boil is an *Orient Express* trick that is safe—you need only worry about live steam surging upward at the end of cooking, not at the beginning as well. Medium heat insures that the water will not boil away too quickly.

BOILING Boiling is probably the easiest cooking method. It was used daily for brewing tea, making soups and stocks, blanching and parboiling raw vegetables for salads, and for performing numerous other chores. Generally the water is unsalted because boiled vegetables and meats are dipped into seasoned sauces afterwards. To speed the boiling process, cover the pot and turn the heat to high.

Steamed Eggs
Light, steamed eggs have the smooth consistency of a custard.

3 large eggs (about
¾ cup)
¾ cup water
½ tablespoon oil
¼ to ½ teaspoon salt

OPTIONAL
sesame oil
Soy Sauce Stock
(p. 4)

PREPARATION: 5 minutes
STEAMING: 15 minutes
UTENSILS: steamer
2-cup measuring cup
heatproof bowl, 6 × 3 inches
fork or chopsticks

STEPS

1. Prepare a steamer.

2. Break the eggs into the measuring cup and add an *equal* volume of water. Add the other ingredients and pour mixture into the heatproof bowl and beat hard for 1 or 2 minutes until delicate bubbles appear on the surface.

3. Put the bowl in the steamer and bring water to a boil.

4. Cover and reduce heat to medium. Steam eggs about 12 minutes or until a fork or chopstick inserted into the center of one comes out clean (no water dripping off its tip). If the eggs are not ready, steam 2 minutes more and retest. For added flavor dribble a couple of drops of sesame oil or 1 teaspoon Soy Sauce Stock on top of the eggs. Serve hot and eat with a spoon.

TIP

You can use a pair of chopsticks to beat the eggs; either the round or square ends will work.

Pork and Bean Curd Balls

MEATBALL MIXTURE

½ pound ground pork
1 bean curd square
2½ tablespoons cornstarch
2 tablespoons water
1 clove garlic, minced
½ teaspoon sherry
½ teaspoon salt

OPTIONAL

parsley

PREPARATION: 10 minutes
STEAMING: 20 minutes
UTENSILS: steamer
plastic bag or clean napkin
mixing bowl
fork or pastry blender
10-inch serving plate
YIELD: 15 meatballs

STEPS

1. Prepare a steamer.
2. With a fork or pastry blender thoroughly combine the meatball mixture; make sure the bean curd is distributed evenly. To make each meatball, firmly press, then roll about 1 tablespoon of the mixture into a ball between your palms. Repeat until you use up all the meat.
3. Place the balls on the plate, ⅜ inches apart; put in the steamer and bring water to a boil.
4. Cover and reduce heat to medium. Steam pork and bean curd balls about 18 minutes or until a fork or chopstick inserted into the center of one comes out clean. Serve hot on a plate ringed with curly, flat-leaf or Chinese parsley.

VARIATION

Add meatballs to 4 cups basic pork stock to make soup.

TIPS

To speed the mincing of the bean curd, put it in a plastic bag or clean cotton napkin and smash it with your palm.

Wet your hands to make shaping the meatballs easier.

Pork and Mushroom Patty

This steamed patty, similar to a hamburger in appearance only, is typical of Chinese home-style cooking.

½ **pound ground pork**
¼ **pound fresh or canned mushrooms, minced**
1 **small egg, beaten**
1 **teaspoon sherry**
1 **teaspoon soy sauce**
1 **teaspoon salt**

PREPARATION: 10 minutes
STEAMING: 20 minutes
UTENSILS: steamer
shallow, heatproof bowl or plate, 6 × 1 inch
fork or chopstick

STEPS

1. Prepare a steamer.
2. With a fork or your fingers thoroughly combine the ingredients. Press the mixture firmly into the plate or shallow, heatproof bowl and flatten and smooth the top with your palm. Make a channel around the patty about ½ inch wide to allow space for liquids to accumulate.
3. Put plate in steamer. Bring water to a boil.
4. Cover and reduce heat to medium. Steam patty about 18 minutes or until a fork or chopstick inserted into its center comes out clean. Pour off excess liquid; cut patty into pielike sections and serve hot.

Steamed Eggplant
Eggplant fanciers will enjoy their favorite vegetable simply steamed and served with dips or a pungent sauce.

1 large or 4 baby eggplants (about 1 pound)

DIPS
¼ cup Soy Sauce Stock (p. 4)
2 to 3 tablespoons oyster sauce

PREPARATION: 5 minutes
STEAMING: 20 minutes
UTENSILS: steamer
small bowls
heatproof plate

VARIATION

Instead of using the dips, combine the following ingredients and pour them over the white flesh of the eggplants after they've been steamed and let the sauce soak in for 2 minutes:

1½ tablespoons soy sauce
1 teaspoon sherry
¼ teaspoon distilled vinegar
¼ teaspoon sesame oil
¼ teaspoon sugar
1 clove garlic, minced

STEPS

1. Wash the eggplant and trim the knobby stem if you use a large one. Cut it in half, lengthwise; then slice each half, lengthwise, into thirds. Cut each third across into halves. The pieces should measure approximately $2 \times 1 \times 1$ inch. If you use the baby eggplants, cut them into quarters, lengthwise.
2. Prepare a steamer.
3. Arrange the eggplant pieces *skin side up* in a circle on the plate; place in the steamer and bring water to a boil. Cover and reduce heat to medium. Steam eggplant for 20 minutes. Remove and drain off any liquid.
4. Serve hot with little bowls or dips or with sauce variation.

TIP
The skin will be tender enough to eat, too.

Szechuan Rice Powder Steaming

Szechuan Province is renowned for its spicy cuisine, yet another of its specialties, Rice Powder Steaming, is virtually unknown to Westerners and deserves more attention. Meats, poultry, and white or sweet potatoes (or taro in China) are steamed in a coating of finely ground rice powder. Plain or seasoned, the rice powder expands during the steaming process to flavor and tenderize the food.

Rice powder is frequently sold in 4 or 5-ounce packets at the meat counters of Chinese markets. English names vary widely: "Steamed Meat Powder" is one. We suggest you use the Chinese characters in the **Shopping List** *at the back of the book. You can make our rice powder mixture at home.*

Homemade Rice Powder Mixture

2 cups uncooked
Cream of Rice
cereal
½ to 1 teaspoon five-
spice powder
1 teaspoon salt

PREPARATION: 2 minutes

STEPS

1. Combine the ingredients.
2. Store in a tightly closed glass jar in a kitchen cabinet for use in Szechuan powder steaming recipes.

TIPS

To insure successful steamed rice powder dishes, note the following tips:

After the food is marinated, combine it with the rice powder mixture in an air-filled plastic bag, at least 15½ × 10½ inches, and shake it until the pieces are well coated.

Pack the food firmly into a well-greased heatproof bowl so that the steamed mold will turn out in an attractive mound. The size of the bowl is important—make sure it is completely filled with food.

After steaming, run the tip of a sharp knife around the rim to loosen the mold a bit. Next, put a plate upside down on top of the bowl. Use a towel to grasp both plate and bowl and turn them upside down.

Check the water level in the steamer from time to time and add boiling water if necessary.

Once you've tried these few simple steps, you'll want to use Szechuan Powder Steaming again and again.

Rice Powder Steamed Pork

1 dried Chinese
  mushroom
1½ pounds lean pork
  loin
½ cup ground rice
  powder or
  homemade rice
  powder mixture
½ tablespoon oil

MARINADE
2 tablespoons soy
  sauce
1 tablespoon sherry
¼ teaspoon salt
¼ teaspoon cayenne
  pepper or ½
  teaspoon red
  pepper flakes
3 cloves garlic,
  minced

PREPARATION: 10 minutes
SOAKING: 20 minutes
MARINATING: 20 minutes
STEAMING: 1½ hours
UTENSILS: steamer
  small bowl
  mixing bowl
  1-quart heatproof bowl
  plastic bag
  10-inch plate

STEPS

1. Soak mushroom in hot water, covered, for 20 minutes. Cut off and discard stem and leave cap whole. Pat dry.
2. Wash and drain pork and cut it into 2 × ½ × ½-inch pieces. Combine the marinade ingredients. Add pork slices, mix well, and marinate for 20 minutes.
3. Prepare a steamer.
4. Put the rice powder in a plastic bag and add half of the pork slices. Trap some air in the bag so that it puffs up. Hold it tightly closed on top and shake the pork and rice mixture until the meat is well coated; add the remaining pork and repeat.
5. Grease a bowl. Put the mushroom cap, black-side down, in the center. Layer the pork strips in the bowl until it is filled. Press them down firmly so the mold holds its shape.
6. Put the bowl in the steamer and bring water to a boil. Cover and reduce heat to medium. Steam pork for 1½ hours or until tender. Carefully remove bowl from steamer, gently tap mold, and turn out onto plate. Serve hot.

Rice Powder Steamed Spareribs

A savory Chinese meat-and-potatoes dish for a chilly winter's eve.

1½ pounds baby pork spareribs, in 2-inch pieces
1 pound all-purpose potatoes or sweet potatoes
½ cup ground rice powder or homemade rice powder mixture
½ tablespoon oil

MARINADE
2 tablespoons soy sauce
1 tablespoon sherry
¼ teaspoon salt
¼ teaspoon black pepper
½ teaspoon red pepper flakes
2 scallions, finely sliced

PREPARATION: 10 minutes
MARINATING: 20 minutes
STEAMING: 2 hours
UTENSILS: steamer
mixing bowl
1½-quart heatproof bowl
plastic bag
10-inch plate

STEPS

1. Wash and drain ribs. Combine the marinade ingredients. Add ribs, mix well, and marinate for 20 minutes.
2. Prepare a steamer.
3. Peel the potatoes and cut into 2 × ½ × ½-inch pieces.
4. Put the rice powder and half the ribs in a plastic bag and shake (see **Step 4** Rice Powder Steamed Pork, p. 56).
5. Grease a bowl. Layer the pork strips in the bowl and layer the potato slices on top. Press them down firmly.
6. Put the bowl in the steamer and bring water to a boil. Cover and reduce heat to medium. Steam ribs and potatoes for 2 hours or until tender. Carefully remove bowl from steamer, gently tap mold, and turn out onto plate. Serve hot.

Steamed New Potatoes, Northern Style
Northern Chinese enjoy these warming new potatoes as snacks dipped in salt and eaten with the fingers.

**1 to 2 pounds new potatoes, 1 to 1½ inches in diameter, unpeeled
salt**

PREPARATION: 2 minutes
STEAMING: 20 minutes
UTENSILS: steamer
fork

STEPS

1. Wash potatoes and place on steamer rack. Bring water to a boil.
2. Reduce heat to medium and steam for 10 minutes. Turn the potatoes over and steam them for 10 minutes more or until they are soft when pricked with a fork or knife.
3. Allow them to cool for a couple of minutes before handling and eating, with or without skin. Serve hot and dip into salt.

"Pearl Balls"
Meatballs take on a new look and flavor when dotted with soft, shiny grains of glutinous rice that swell during steaming.

PREPARATION: 20 minutes
SOAKING: 2 hours
STEAMING: 30 minutes
UTENSILS: 2 small bowls
colander
towel
steamer
mixing bowl
fork
heatproof plate
YIELD: 20 meatballs

⅔ cup glutinous rice

MEATBALL MIXTURE
1 pound ground beef or ½ pound ground beef plus ½ pound ground pork
4 dried Chinese mushrooms
1 scallion, very finely sliced
1 teaspoon ginger, minced
1 tablespoon soy sauce
1½ teaspoons salt
½ teaspoon sugar

OPTIONAL
1 egg, lightly beaten
6 canned water chestnuts, minced

STEPS

1. In a small bowl cover the rice with water and soak for 2 hours. Drain well and spread grains out on a clean towel to dry. (See **Tips,** Rice Porridge with Ground Beef or Chicken, p. 31.)

2. Soak mushrooms in hot water, covered, for 20 minutes. Drain. Cut off stems and discard. Mince caps.

3. Prepare a steamer.

4. With a fork or your fingers thoroughly combine the ingredients for the meatballs in a mixing bowl. To make each meatball, firmly press, then roll 1 tablespoon of the mixture into a ball between your palms. Repeat until all the meat is used up. (Moistening your hands from time to time with water makes it easier to form meatballs.)

5. Gently press and roll the balls against the rice so the grains stick to the meatballs and cover them. Place on heatproof plate leaving space between meatballs. Put in steamer. Bring water to a boil. Reduce heat to medium and steam, covered, for 25 or 30 minutes. Check water level during steaming. Serve hot.

VARIATION

Peel ½ pound sweet potatoes and cut into ½-inch rounds. Place them underneath the meatballs in the heatproof bowl. You'll have a starch to go with the meal and the bright orange makes festive company fare.

Steamed Duck

Steamed duck is quite different from roast duck. It's lean because liquids and fat globules drip out during steaming. The duck meat is smooth and satiny and melts in your mouth.

4 to 5-pound duckling with giblets, preferably fresh
¼ cup sherry
¼ cup salt

PREPARATION: 5 minutes
SALTING: 3 hours to overnight
STEAMING: 1½ hours or more
UTENSILS: plastic bag large enough for duck and giblets
9-inch pie pan or roasting pan, 11 × 7 inches
steamer or roasting pan, 16 × 12½ × 7½ inches with cover
bulb baster
heatproof 1-quart bowl or 4-cup measuring cup
long-handled spoon
oval serving platter

STEPS

1. If the duckling is frozen, remove the outer wrapper and thaw it at room temperature for 10 to 12 hours.
2. Wash giblets. Wash duck inside and out. Evenly distribute the sherry and the salt over the giblets and on the skin of the duck as well as inside its cavity. Rub the salt in; it flavors the duck. Put the duck and giblets in a plastic bag in the refrigerator for 3 hours to overnight.
3. Prepare a steamer.
4. Place duck, *breast side up,* in the pie pan or roasting pan and arrange the giblets on either side. Bring water to a boil. Turn heat to medium and steam duck, covered, for ½ hour.
5. Remove the liquid that accumulates in the pan with a bulb baster. Squeeze it into a bowl or measuring cup and cool. Check water level in steamer. Add more boiling water if necessary. Cover duck and steam for ½ hour more. Withdraw more liquid and check water level again. Turn duck over and steam for final ½ hour or until meat is tender. Poke the end of a chopstick into the leg; the juice should be clear, not pink.

6. Place a long-handled spoon in its cavity and carefully lift duck out. After placing it on a warmed platter, cut 4-inch long, criss-cross slashes on the breast to make it easier to lift the meat off with a fork or chopsticks. Or you may cut the duck in half, lengthwise, down its center; then cut it across into 2 × 1-inch pieces.

7. Pour any remaining duck liquid into a bowl or measuring cup and cool it. You should have approximately 4 cups. Reserve liquid for use as Duck Fat (p. 121) and Duck Stock.

8. Slice the gizzard, heart, and liver into ¼-inch slivers and place them in a ring around the duck. Serve hot.

TIP

Serve half the duck and save the other half for Crispy Duck (p. 165). Leftover Steamed Duck makes good sandwiches and keeps 1 week.

Steamed Flounder with Black Beans

If you've never prepared whole steamed fish before, this dish is a good one to try. It's a classic that blends the sweetness of the flounder or sea bass with a medley of pungent black beans, ginger, and scallions. In China, fish symbolizes wealth.

1½ to 2-pound flounder or sea bass, with head and tail
2 to 3 teaspoons salt
2 tablespoons sherry
5 slices ginger, 1 × 1 × ¼ inch
3 scallions, in 1 × ⅛-inch shreds

SAUCE
1 tablespoon fermented black beans
1 tablespoon soy sauce
½ tablespoon sherry
1 tablespoon oil

OPTIONAL
¼ cup carrots, in 1 × ⅛-inch shreds

PREPARATION: 15 minutes
MARINATING: 15 minutes
STEAMING: 15 to 20 minutes
UTENSILS: paper towels
small bowl
steamer
rimmed oval platter, 12 × 9 inches

STEPS

1. Wash flounder or sea bass in cold water and pat dry. Cut 5 slashes, 1 inch apart, across the fat part of the dark side, each about 3 inches long and ½ inch deep.

2. Sprinkle salt over the outside of the fish and in its gills and cavity, rubbing it in gently with your fingers. Pour sherry on top and marinate for 15 minutes. Rinse fish in cold water and pat dry.

3. Cut each of the 5 ginger pieces in half. Into each slash push two pieces of ginger, side by side. Put fish on the platter.

4. Prepare a steamer.

5. Combine sauce ingredients and pour over the middle of the fish. Sprinkle shreds of scallions and carrots on top. Put fish in steamer and bring water to a boil. Reduce heat to medium and steam fish, covered, for 15 to 20 minutes. Do not overcook. Test for doneness by poking a chopstick into the thickest part. The meat should be white and separate easily from the bone. Serve hot at once.

The skin of the fish should be completely free of scales. Double check by running your fingers over both sides. If the skin feels rough anywhere, remove the remaining scales by rubbing a serrated knife against them. Rinse fish and pat dry.

If you prefer not to serve the fish with the head, remove it before steaming.

Honeyed Ham, Hunan Style
This dish is an adaptation of a regional specialty from China's central Hunan Province, which is renowned for its ham. Slices of pork butt in a honey-wine-and-sugar syrup are steamed and tucked into absorbent Steamed Buns or Steamed Bread packets.

1   to 1½-pound boneless smoked pork shoulder butt
1   glazed or maraschino cherry

SYRUP
1   tablespoon honey
2   tablespoons sherry
1   tablespoon sugar

SAUCE
1   teaspoon cornstarch
¼   cup water
⅓   cup liquid from steamed pork

PREPARATION: 15 minutes
COOKING: 45 minutes
STEAMING: 30 minutes
UTENSILS: 3-quart saucepan with lid
long-handled fork
steamer
heatproof bowl or mold, 6 × 3 inches
small saucepan
dish or pan cover slightly smaller than the heat-proof bowl
wooden spoon
2-inch deep serving dish
towel

STEPS

1. Remove outside advertising wrapper and leave inner plastic, paper, or net wrapper on shoulder butt. If it is uncooked, follow the instructions on the wrapper or cover ham with water in the larger saucepan. Put lid on and bring to a boil.

2. Reduce heat to medium and simmer for 30 minutes. Turn meat over and simmer 10 to 15 minutes more. Remove from water, cut off inner wrapper, and cool. Slice into $2 \times 1 \times \frac{1}{4}$-inch pieces.

3. Prepare a steamer.

4. Put the cherry in the center of the heatproof bowl and carefully overlap meat slices in a neat circle around it. Next, layer the meat slices up the sides of the bowl, then fill the center, and finally, press the meat slices down firmly so the mold will hold its shape.

5. Combine honey, wine, and sugar and pour over meat slices.

6. Put the bowl in the steamer and bring water to a brisk boil. Reduce heat to medium and steam, covered, for 30 minutes.

7. Carefully remove bowl. To pour off liquid from ham, place a dish or pan cover slightly smaller than the bowl over it. Securely grasp both with a heavy towel and pour off the liquid, reserving $\frac{1}{3}$ cup in a small saucepan. Bring the reserved liquid to a boil. Combine the cornstarch and water. While stirring constantly, add cornstarch mixture to boiling liquid; continue stirring until it thickens. Remove from heat.

8. Place serving plate upside down over bowl and quickly turn ham out. Pour sauce over it. Serve hot with Steamed Buns (p. 42) or Steamed Bread.

PREPARE AHEAD: Steps 1 through **5** can be done 1 day before—keep in refrigerator.

Steamed Bread

Steaming white bread gives it a soft, but not soggy, texture. It's best arranged like petals on a large platter around Honeyed Ham, Hunan Style (p. 63), Crispy Duck (p. 165), or with Steamed Chinese Sausage (p. 141). Slip bite-size pieces of meat into each bread envelope for a miniature sandwich.

4 slices white bread

PREPARATION: 3 minutes
STEAMING: 5 minutes
UTENSILS: steamer
wax paper

STEPS

1. Trim the crusts and slice pieces of bread in half into rectangles. Slice each piece ¾ of the way through but leave one short side attached.
2. Prepare a steamer. Line the rack or support with wax paper. Bring water to a boil and place bread slices on the wax paper. Reduce heat to medium and steam bread 5 minutes.
3. To remove, lift wax paper up by the corners and turn bread out. Serve immediately as the bread cools rapidly.

TIP

To make it easier to slice the bread, freeze it first. Allow it to thaw and soften a bit, then slice.

Boiled Spinach

This simply cooked spinach is enjoyed in China as light summer fare that is neither fried nor oily.

1 pound fresh spinach
4 to 6 cups water

SUBSTITUTE
For fresh spinach use
2 10-ounce packages
of frozen whole leaf
spinach.

DIP A
2 tablespoons oyster
sauce

DIP B
1 tablespoon soy sauce
plus ½ tablespoon
sesame oil

PREPARATION: 5 minutes
COOKING: 10 minutes
UTENSILS: 3-quart saucepan with lid
slotted spoon
colander

STEPS

1. Bring water to a boil. Wash fresh spinach well and pull stems apart; use the pink ends, too. Put spinach in pan and stir over high heat for 4 to 5 minutes until the water comes to a boil again.
2. Drain and cut into 2-inch pieces.
3. Mix soy sauce and sesame oil for Dip B.
4. Serve spinach hot, cold, or at room temperature with dips in small bowls.

TIP

After cooking, the spinach should be a deep, bright green; do not overcook it.

Boiled *Bok Choy*

In the Cantonese dialect bok choy means "white vegetable." Above its white stems are round, dark green leaves and sometimes clusters of tiny, bright yellow flowers. (Pinch off these flower stalks and pop them into a small bud vase.) Bok choy is native to South China but can be bought by the pound in Oriental food markets any time of year. When boiled, it glistens and looks like white and green jade.

1 pound *bok choy*
6 cups water

DIP A
2 tablespoons oyster sauce

DIP B
1 tablespoon soy sauce plus 1 tablespoon sesame oil

PREPARATION: 5 minutes
COOKING: 5 minutes
UTENSILS: 3-quart saucepan with lid
slotted spoon
colander

STEPS

1. Bring water to a boil. Trim root end of *bok choy* and wash. Cut white stalks in half, lengthwise, from the base and cut stalks and leaves into 1½-inch pieces.
2. Add cut pieces to pan and bring to boil again. Let boil for 2 minutes, stirring once or twice. Drain.
3. Mix soy sauce and sesame oil for Dip B.
4. Serve *bok choy* hot with dips in small bowls.

TIP

Arrange the cooked vegetable by mounding the dark green leaves in the center of the serving plate with the white stalks petal-fashion around them. The dish will appeal to the eye as well as to the palate.

Salads and Pickles

Salads or pickles are an integral part of the Chinese diet. A homemade supply is usually on hand to be served at breakfast and later at family-style meals with hot dishes, soup, and plain rice or buns. Besides providing a source of vitamins, they add color, taste, and texture to the dining experience.

Chinese and Western salads have little in common. Western salads are generally raw, soft, leafy greens tossed with any one of a number of different dressings. By contrast, Chinese salads are often firm-textured vegetables that have been blanched or parboiled. After chilling, they are lightly coated with either a blend of soy sauce, sesame oil or vinegar, salt, and sugar, or with sesame paste.

An Oriental salad usually consists of only one vegetable—asparagus, cucumbers, radishes, or bean sprouts—served on a single, communal plate from which the diners help themselves with chopsticks. Despite occasional accents of minced ginger, scallions, or Szechuan mustard pickle, Chinese salads are characteristically simple and crisp.

A favorite daily food of the Chinese peasant is a bowl of rice with a few pieces of homemade pickle. A wide variety of vegetables are pickled in brine during the seasons in which they grow and then are stored in cool, dark places. Cabbages, cauliflower, cucumbers, turnips, ginger, broccoli, peppers, and string beans are but a few examples. Different parts of these vegetables are used: roots, stems, skins, leaves, and tubers.

Salads and Pickles

In farms throughout China, home pickling products were used to supplement the meal. Each family had its own secret pickling recipe and enjoyed giving its pickles as presents to friends, neighbors, and relatives.

Szechuan-style pickles (*p'ao t'sai*), which we tell you how to make, are especially famous; they are usually hot, crunchy, and loved by everyone. They are a very simple and enjoyable means of adding bright, zesty pickles made from familiar Western vegetables to your table. Serve them as accompaniments to both Eastern and Western meals.

Asparagus Salad
This simple salad is a pretty dish for spring when fresh asparagus is plentiful and less expensive.

1 **pound fresh asparagus**
6 **cups water**

DRESSING
1½ **tablespoons soy sauce**
1 **teaspoon sesame oil**
¼ **teaspoon sugar**
⅛ **teaspoon salt**

PREPARATION: 15 minutes
CHILLING: 20 minutes
UTENSILS: 3-quart saucepan with lid
colander
paper towels
small bowl

STEPS

1. Bend the bottom of each asparagus stalk so that 1 to 2 inches of the tough, woody end snaps off. Discard. Scrape off the pale pink scales along the stalk. Wash asparagus and drain.

2. Bring water to a rapid boil.

3. Cut the stalks at a 45° slant into 1½-inch pieces. Put them into the boiling water and parboil 1 to 2 minutes until the skins turn bright green. Remove immediately and put under cold running water until they cool. Pat them dry and chill in the refrigerator for 20 minutes.

4. Just before serving, mix the dressing ingredients and pour over asparagus. Toss gently and serve cold.

TIP

When buying asparagus, pick the narrower stalks, not the fatter, woody ones. Press a nail into the bottom of the stalk to see if it is tender or tough. The tips should be compact and upright, not loose and wilted. Tender, young asparagus will taste much better than tough, older ones in this barely cooked dish.

Bean Curd Salad
Bland bean curd cubes mingle with pungent bits of ginger and spicy Szechuan mustard pickle in an interesting, thoroughly Chinese salad.

1   **pound bean curd**
2   **cups water**
4   **teaspoons salt**
1   **tablespoon scallion greens, finely sliced**

OPTIONAL
1½ **tablespoons Szechuan mustard pickle, minced**
1   **teaspoon ginger, minced**

DRESSING
1½ **tablespoons sesame oil**
1   **tablespoon soy sauce**
½ **teaspoon sugar**
¼ **teaspoon salt**

PREPARATION: 10 minutes
SALTING AND CHILLING: 20 minutes
UTENSILS: 1-quart saucepan with lid
shallow bowl
paper towels
small bowl

STEPS

1. Bring water to a boil, pour over bean curd, and let sit for 1 minute. Drain bean curd and rinse under cold running water for 2 minutes until it cools.

2. Cut bean curd into 1-inch cubes and sprinkle with the salt. Chill in refrigerator for 20 minutes. Pour off any liquid and carefully pat cubes dry with paper towels.

3. Sprinkle bean curd with scallions and, if you use them, ginger and Szechuan mustard pickle.

4. Mix the dressing ingredients, pour over salad, mix gently, and serve cold at once.

VARIATION

Replace the dressing with 2 tablespoons of oyster sauce and pour over the salad.

TIP

Lightly seasoned bean curd and scallions are delicious alone; adding ginger and Szechuan mustard pickle alters the taste, texture, and appearance of the dish dramatically. Try it plain, then fancy.

Bean Sprout Salad
Crisp white bean sprouts, green scallions, and red peppers or radishes make a pleasing tricolor combination. A touch of red symbolizes happiness for a Chinese household.

½ pound fresh bean
sprouts
4 cups water
1 tablespoon
scallions, finely
sliced
2 tablespoons red
bell pepper, finely
diced or 3 red
radishes, in ¼-inch
slices

DRESSING
1 tablespoon soy
sauce
½ tablespoon distilled
white vinegar
½ tablespoon sesame
oil
¼ teaspoon salt

OPTIONAL
⅛ teaspoon sugar

PREPARATION: 10 minutes
CHILLING: 20 minutes
UTENSILS: 3-quart saucepan with lid
colander
small bowl

STEPS

1. Bring water to a boil, remove saucepan from heat, add the bean sprouts, and let sit for 1 to 2 minutes. Drain bean sprouts and rinse well under cold running water.
2. Chill the vegetables in the refrigerator for 20 minutes.
3. Mix the dressing ingredients, pour over vegetables, and toss gently. Serve cold.

TIP

Soaking the bean sprouts in boiling water improves their taste and texture, while rinsing them under cold water cleanses and freshens them.

Sweet "n" Sour Chinese Cabbage

Chinese cabbage (Napa) is the most abundant winter vegetable in Peking and other northern parts of China. Traditionally, before the first snows fell, a large family might order 50 or 60 of this crinkly leafed vegetable, totaling 200 pounds or more! During this season it was eaten every day—in soups, salads, buns, and dumplings, quick fried or pickled.

The cabbages were left outside in the cold near the kitchen. The huge pile was commonly covered with a hemp rug that allowed air to circulate, kept the moisture in, and protected the cabbages from drying out under the sun. Frost and snow did not harm these hardy vegetables; they were simply thawed.

If the family had an outdoor, raised brick gold-fish pond, the cabbages might be heaped there while the delicate fan-tailed fish resided inside the house. The fish stayed there, safe and snug in pottery or bronze tubs, until warm weather arrived and the cabbages were gone.

Sweet "n" Sour Chinese Cabbage is a wintertime favorite in the North when both the cabbages and radishes are in season. We predict it will become a year-round favorite of yours.

PREPARATION: 15 minutes
SALTING AND CHILLING: 20 minutes
UTENSILS: 2-quart wide-mouthed glass jar or plastic container with tightly fitting lid
heavy bottle or can

1½ to 2-pound Chinese
    cabbage (Napa)
½ teaspoon salt
    plus
1   teaspoon salt
½ cup red bell pepper,
    shredded
6   small red radishes

DRESSING
½ tablespoon dry
    sherry
½ tablespoon distilled
    white vinegar
½ tablespoon sesame
    oil
1   tablespoon sugar

STEPS

1. Trim root end of cabbage and discard. Remove the tough outer leaves and save them for use in Duck Bone Soup (p. 123) and Meatball Soup (p. 128). Reserve about 1 pound of the tender inner leaves and stalks, cutting them *across* the fat part into ¼-inch pieces.

2. Place half of the cabbage and ½ teaspoon salt into the 2-quart jar or plastic container. Close it securely and shake it up and down vigorously a few times. Then turn the container completely upside down, once. Upright the container, remove the lid, and add the remaining cabbage and 1 teaspoon salt. Repeat the shaking and let rest for 5 minutes. Shake once again. (The shaking helps distribute the salt, which will eventually wilt and flavor the cabbage.)

3. Mix the dressing ingredients and add to the container with the shredded red pepper. Mix, shake, and put in the refrigerator. Occasionally shake (2 or 3 times) until the cabbage wilts to half its original volume (about 20 minutes).

4. Trim the ends of the radishes and wash them. To lightly crack each radish, put it on its round side. Pound it hard, once, with a heavy bottle or can. Add the cracked radishes to the container and mix with other vegetables. To serve, first remove the vegetables and then ladle a bit of liquid on top. Serve cold.

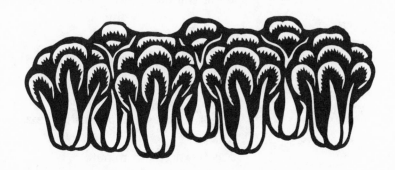

Celery Salad
This combination of celery and meat, poultry, or seafood tossed in a sesame oil-soy sauce duo makes a refreshing summer luncheon salad.

1   pound celery
½   cup chilled cooked ham, shredded, or ½ cup chilled canned baby clams, drained, plus 2 teaspoons clam juice

OPTIONAL
1   cup chilled cooked chicken breast, shredded

DRESSING
1   teaspoon sesame oil
½   teaspoon soy sauce
½   teaspoon salt

PREPARATION: 15 minutes
CHILLING: 20 minutes
UTENSILS: colander
small bowl

STEPS

1. Trim leaves and white ends of celery stalks. Break stalks in half and pull strings out from broken edges. Wash, drain, and chill in refrigerator for 20 minutes. Cut the stalks at a 45° slant into 2 × ¼-inch pieces.
2. Mix the dressing ingredients. Combine the celery with either ham, clams and clam juice, or with chicken (see **Tip**).
3. Pour the dressing on top of the salad; toss gently to coat and serve cold.

TIP

To cook the chicken, cover half a breast with boiling water and cook for 10 minutes. Drain and chill in refrigerator for 20 minutes. Before serving, pull the meat and skin apart with your fingers into 1 × ⅜-inch pieces. Pulling it apart in this manner is preferred by a Chinese cook to cutting it with a knife; it has a more natural look.

"Cellophane" Noodle Salad
This dish is a colorful medley of shredded vegetables and transparent "cellophane" noodles that offers delicate tastes and interesting textures.

PREPARATION: 15 minutes
UTENSILS: 1-quart saucepan with lid
colander
small bowl
peeler

2 ounces
  "cellophane"
  noodles
2 cups water
1 cup celery
¼ pound carrots

OPTIONAL
¼ cup red bell pepper,
  shredded
¼ pound cooked ham,
  shredded

DRESSING
1½ tablespoons soy
  sauce
1 tablespoon sesame
  oil
1 teaspoon salt
½ teaspoon sugar

STEPS

1. Bring water to a boil. Remove from heat. Add "cellophane" noodles to water and let sit *only* 1 to 2 minutes until they soften and separate. Drain and immediately rinse noodles under cold running water for 1 or 2 minutes until cool. Drain and cut into 2-inch pieces.

2. Trim leaves and white ends of celery stalks. Break stalks in half and pull strings out from broken edges. Wash and drain. Cut the stalks at a 45° slant into 2 × ¼-inch pieces.

3. Peel carrots. Slant-slice them into 2 × ¼-inch ovals; then carefully cut into 1 × ⅛-inch shreds.

4. Mix the dressing ingredients. To serve, mound the noodles in the center of a plate and arrange the carrots, celery, pepper, and ham in rings around it. Pour dressing over salad, bring it to the table immediately, and gently toss it before your guests. Serve at room temperature.

TIPS

Do not refrigerate leftover salad as the "cellophane" noodles will become hard.

For an easy way to get pretty carrot shreds, use the large opening of a grater.

In North China "cellophane" noodles are called "winter" noodles, while in the South they are called "silky" noodles. In this country "cellophane" noodles are also called "transparent" noodles or "bean threads." They are translucent and resemble nylon sewing thread. Made from mung bean starch and water, they are usually sold in 2-ounce packets, sometimes packaged in groups of 10. These versatile noodles keep indefinitely and are wonderful to have on hand—they can go into soups, salads, and quick-fried dishes, or they can be deep fried into celestial white puffs. Look for these noodles in Oriental groceries.

Sweet "n" Sour Cucumber Salad

Cucumbers grown in North China are much more delicate in appearance and taste than the fat, thick-skinned ones we know. They are seedless and only about 1 inch across. They are also one of the few vegetables eaten raw (skin and all) with salt or a sauce or prepared as a salad.

2   **medium cucumbers**
2   **cups water**

DRESSING
2   **tablespoons soy sauce**
2   **teaspoons red wine vinegar**
2   **teaspoons sugar**
½   **teaspoon salt**

PREPARATION: 5 minutes
SCALDING: 15 minutes
CHILLING: 15 minutes
UTENSILS: 1-quart saucepan with lid
peeler
spoon
colander
small bowls

STEPS

1. Trim ends of cucumbers and discard. Peel each cucumber by leaving alternating strips of dark green skin, about ⅜ inch wide, down its length. Cut each cucumber in half, lengthwise, scoop out the seeds, and cut each half, lengthwise, again; then cut *across* into pieces approximately 1 × 1½ inches.
2. Bring water to a boil. Remove from heat.
3. Add cucumber pieces to boiling water and let sit for 15 minutes. (Scalding the cucumbers in boiling water gives them a crispy texture.) Drain and soak under cold running water until cool (you can add a couple of ice cubes to speed the process).
4. Mix the dressing ingredients and pour over cucumbers. Chill in refrigerator for 15 minutes. Toss gently to coat before serving.

TIP

Buy thin, bumpy-skinned cucumbers. These will be more tender than fat, smooth-skinned cucumbers.

Cucumbers with Sesame Paste

If you're a peanut butter fan, you'll like the taste of sesame paste in this unusual and pleasant combination.

2 medium cucumbers
1 tablespoon salt

DRESSING
1 tablespoon sesame paste
or 1 tablespoon smooth-style peanut butter
1 tablespoon soy sauce
1 tablespoon sesame oil

OPTIONAL
1 clove garlic, minced

PREPARATION: 5 minutes
CHILLING: 10 minutes
UTENSILS: peeler
spoon
paper towels
small bowl

STEPS

1. Trim ends of cucumbers and discard. Peel each cucumber by leaving alternating strips of dark green skin, about ⅜ inch wide, down its length. Cut each cucumber in half, lengthwise, scoop out the seeds, and cut each half, lengthwise, again; then cut *across* into pieces approximately 1 × 1½ inches.

2. Rub salt into cucumber pieces with your fingers and chill in refrigerator for 10 minutes. Rinse with cold water and pat dry.

3. Mix the dressing ingredients and pour over cucumbers just bèfore serving. Toss gently to coat.

TIP

Do not refrigerate the salad after you've added the sesame paste, because the sesame oil in it will congeal.

Radish Salad *The tartness of these radishes is only lightly veiled by an Oriental dressing of sesame oil and soy sauce.*

1½ cups red radishes
1   teaspoon salt

DRESSING
1   tablespoon soy
    sauce
1   teaspoon vinegar
1   teaspoon sugar
    sesame oil

PREPARATION: 5 minutes
SALTING AND CHILLING: 15 minutes
UTENSILS: small bowls
heavy bottle or can
paper towels

STEPS

1. Trim the ends of the radishes and wash them. To crack each radish, put it on its round side. Pound it once, hard, with a heavy bottle or can until the radish splits open.
2. Rub salt into radish pieces with your fingers and chill in refrigerator for 15 minutes. Rinse off the salt and pat dry.
3. Mix the dressing ingredients, pour over the radishes, and stir gently. Just before serving add 2 or 3 drops of sesame oil.

TIP

The salt eliminates some of the bitterness from the radishes and also crisps and flavors them.

Salted Broccoli Stems

Do not discard broccoli stems. When salted and thinly sliced, Chinese style, they become an economical complement to any meat or poultry dish.

1 pound broccoli stems (use florets for Quick-Fried Broccoli, p. 102)
2 teaspoons salt

OPTIONAL
sesame oil

PREPARATION: 10 minutes
CHILLING: 4 to 8 hours
UTENSILS: bowl or plastic container with tightly fitting lid

STEPS

1. Make a small cut in the bottom of each broccoli stem and peel off about ⅛ inch of the outer skin; slowly pull it up and away to expose the tender, whitish green flesh beneath. Trim knobs and dark green leaves and discard.
2. Cut the stems into 2-inch chunks. Mix them with the salt, put in a bowl or plastic container, cover tightly, and shake up and down for 1 minute to distribute the salt. Put stems in refrigerator for 4 to 8 hours.
3. Remove broccoli, rinse off the salt, and slice stems into ¼-inch diagonal pieces. For a nutty flavor, trickle a couple of drops of sesame oil on top. Serve cold.

TIPS

The longer you leave the salted broccoli stems in the refrigerator the saltier they'll get. After 4 hours slice a piece off, rinse it in cold water, and taste it. If you prefer it saltier, leave it for another 4 hours or so.

If you wish to keep the stems for a couple of days, rinse the salt off first.

PREPARE AHEAD: 2 to 3 days.

Three Pickles: String Beans and Carrots, White Cabbage and Red Peppers, Cauliflower and Carrots

Once you master this easy home-style pickling method, you'll use it again and again to make delicious and attractive pickled vegetables. Pass the goodness along; Chinese families often exchange jars of their homemade pickles.

 GOOD FOR BEGINNERS

String Beans and Carrots

¾ **pound fresh string beans**
2 **ounces carrots**
2 **slices ginger**

PICKLING BRINE
3 **cups water**
1½ **tablespoons salt**
1 **tablespoon gin, vodka, or Scotch whisky**
1 **tablespoon sugar**
¼ or ½ **teaspoon whole black peppercorns**

PREPARATION: 10 minutes
PICKLING: 2 to 3 days
UTENSILS: 1-quart glass jar with lid
peeler
4-cup measuring cup
3-inch square of wax paper
fork or chopsticks

STEPS

1. Snap off the ends of the string beans. Wash and drain well. Peel carrots. At a 45° slant, cut them into ⅜-inch ovals. With a fork or chopsticks push the vegetables and ginger slices into the jar.

2. Combine the pickling brine ingredients and stir to completely dissolve the salt and sugar. Pour the brine slowly into the jar so that the vegetables are *completely submerged.*

3. Put the square of wax paper over the mouth of the jar and screw the lid on. Leave the jar in a cool, shady spot where air circulates—basement, cellar, wine cellar, open closet—for 2 days. Open the jar slowly and taste the pickling brine with a clean spoon. If it has the taste of pickle juice and you are satisfied with it, put the jar in the refrigerator; when chilled the pickles are ready to eat. However, if you prefer a stronger brine, leave the jar in a cool place 1 day longer. Serve chilled.

White Cabbage and Red Peppers

½ pound white
   cabbage
1 red bell pepper
2 slices ginger

PREPARATION: 15 minutes

STEPS

1. Remove the tough outer leaves and cut out the hard white core and discard. Cut the cabbage into quarters and then into 2-inch wedges. Cut each pepper in half, lengthwise, clean out the seeds and whitish pith, and cut into 1-inch square·pieces. Push the vegetables and ginger slices into the jar and follow **Steps 2** and **3** above. (You can replace the peppercorns with red pepper flakes for a Szechuan spiciness.)

Cauliflower and Carrots

¾ pound cauliflower
   florets, trimmed
2 ounces carrots
2 slices ginger

PREPARATION: 20 minutes

STEPS

1. Trim woody ends of cauliflower stems. To remove florets, first cut the stem up to the bottom of each floret and then break it away carefully with your fingers. (This method will keep the florets whole and neat.) Next, pare away the tough outer skin from the stems of the florets. Make a cut in the bottom and peel off about ⅛ inch of the outer skin; slowly pull it up and away to expose the tender flesh beneath.

2. Peel carrots. Slant-slice them into ⅜-inch ovals. Push the vegetables and ginger slices into the jar and follow **Steps 2** and **3** of the String Beans and Carrots recipe.

TIPS

When adding or removing vegetables from the jar, always use a clean, dry utensil—never your fingers—so the brine doesn't become contaminated.

When opening the jar for the first time, open it *slowly*. If there is any bubbling or fizzing from the liquid near the mouth of the jar, it is a *natural by-product* of the fermentation of the pickling brine. Clouding of the liquid is also natural.

If after a week the pickled vegetables are not eaten, remove them from the brine and transfer to a jar or plastic container with cap. They will keep indefinitely. Use some of the pickled string beans in Beef with Pickled String Beans (p. 106).

Do not discard the pickling brine. Use it again and add dry, hard vegetables. To fill the jar with additional fresh brine, use a smaller amount of each ingredient in the same proportions called for in the recipe.

It is important that the vegetables are completely submerged in the pickling brine. You may want to add a couple of clean pebbles to weigh down the vegetables.

PREPARE AHEAD: up to 1 week in pickling brine; indefinitely when removed from brine.

Mixed Pickled Vegetables, Szechuan Style
Red pepper flakes in the pickling brine make this dish spicier in the manner of Szechuan Province.

1 large carrot
½ pound white cabbage
1 cucumber (about ½ pound)
1 red bell pepper (about ¼ pound)
1 green bell pepper (about ¼ pound)
4 slices ginger

PICKLING BRINE

6 cups water
3 tablespoons salt
2 tablespoons gin, vodka, or Scotch whisky
2 tablespoons sugar
1 teaspoon red pepper flakes

PREPARATION: 30 minutes
PICKLING: 2 to 3 days
UTENSILS: 1 wide-mouth, 2-quart jar or 2 wide-mouth, 1-quart jars with lids
peeler
4-cup measuring cup
2 3-inch squares of wax paper
fork or chopsticks

STEPS

1. Peel carrots and slant-slice them into ¼-inch ovals. Prepare cabbage as in Pickled White Cabbage and Red Peppers (p. 85), and cut into 4 × 3-inch wedges. Trim ends of cucumbers and discard. Cut each cucumber in half, lengthwise; scoop out the seeds and cut each half into 4 pieces, lengthwise, then across into 2-inch pieces. (Do not peel the cucumbers.) Cut each pepper in half, lengthwise, clean out the seeds and whitish pith, and cut into ⅜-inch slices.

2. Divide the vegetables and pickling brine into two equal parts. Into each jar push the cabbage in first, the carrots next, then the peppers, and the cucumbers last. Add the ginger slices and cover completely with the pickling brine. Press them all down firmly. Follow **Steps 2** and **3** of the String Beans and Carrots recipe.

TIP

Eat the softer cucumbers and peppers first and then eat the firmer-textured carrots, cabbage, and ginger slices.

Cooking with Oil

QUICK FRYING and DEEP FRYING

QUICK FRYING AND DEEP FRYING

Cooking oil is essential to the Chinese cook. Small amounts are used for quick frying and larger quantities are recycled for deep frying. Oil reaches a high temperature quickly and seals in the natural flavor and juices of foods.

The Chinese chef either chooses solid animal fats—fat from chickens or ducks, and lard from pigs—or liquid oils from vegetables—oil from peanuts, soybeans, and sesame seeds. Recipes in this book, however, have been tested with corn or vegetable oils. (Butter and olive oil are too strongly flavored.) Always use fresh, new oil.

Stir frying

This method is well known in Chinese-American restaurants, because the cook stirs the food in a *wok* without a cover. Stir frying emphasizes speed. Because the foods are precut, the preparation time is usually 2 to 3 times longer than the cooking time.

Meats are thinly sliced and must be cooked rapidly so they don't overcook and become tough. Vegetables are often cut the same size and have to be moved constantly around the pan so they become coated with oil but don't lose their crisp texture or burn. Stir frying requires more skill and split-second timing than cooking with soy sauce or water.

Cooking with Oil

Orient Express
Quick frying

Quick frying is similar to stir frying, but it doesn't require a *wok*, the round-bottomed Chinese cooking pot. Many Chinese-Americans do not own one. If you have a *wok*, by all means use it; just subtract 1 tablespoon of oil from each quick-fry recipe.

To perfect your quick frying, follow these steps:

1. Heat the pan over high heat for 20 seconds.
2. Heat the oil over medium-high heat for 20 to 30 seconds.
3. Quickly add the food. Cover the pan and shake it over the heat for 10 seconds only, until the sizzling stops.
4. Remove the lid. Stir the food constantly in a circular motion to bring it up from the bottom.

The size and material of the saucepan is important. There must be room for the foods to be stirred, turned, coated with oil, and combined with seasonings. The heat should be evenly distributed. We recommend a 3-quart stainless steel or aluminum saucepan with a tight-fitting lid and a sturdy handle that doesn't conduct heat. This type of saucepan should work well for all quick-fry recipes using the cover-shake-stir method. A long-handled spoon, with or without perforations or slots, will also be needed.

Everything involved in frying, including the pan and spoon, should be as dry as possible for a minimum of splattering so the oil can do its job immediately. Vegetables should be washed and drained in a colander in advance (preferably an hour ahead) or carefully patted dry first.

OIL

The time needed to bring the oil to the right temperature will vary; it depends on the pan you use as well as the type of heat—gas or electric. The oil should have a light haze over it, but no smoke. If the oil smokes, it is too hot; turn the heat off, cover the pan, and let it cool for a few moments. If the oil is too hot it will burn the food, especially the vegetables. If it is too cold, meats will stick to the pan and not heat through. Only experience will teach you just when the oil is ready, and the same is true for the finished dish. Vegetables should reach their brightest hue; when overcooked they start looking dull, become soft, and lose their crisp texture. Ideally, quick-fried foods should be served hot and eaten right away. Unlike stewed, steamed, or deep-fried dishes, they cannot wait for the diner.

Deep Frying

Deep-fried foods are common in North China, especially during the winter months. The method is the same as that used in our Western kitchens.

Follow these steps to deep fry foods the *Orient Express* way:

1. Heat the pan over medium heat for 20 seconds.
2. Heat the oil over medium heat 3 to 5 minutes.
3. Add the foods and turn them over to cook evenly.
4. Lift out the foods and drain on paper towels.

Choose a 3-quart saucepan (with or without a metal deep-fry basket), skillet, electric deep fryer, or 14-inch *wok*. You will need a long-handled slotted spoon (or wire skimmer) and paper towels.

Deep-fried foods should not be heavy or greasy. They can sometimes be warmed up the next day in a 250° oven for 10 minutes.

When deep frying open your kitchen windows and shut doors so rooms don't fill up with an oily odor. If you have an exhaust fan in your cooking area, be sure to use it.

OIL

How much oil should you use? There should be 2 to 3 inches of oil in your pan, enough to immerse the foods (approximately 2 to 3 cups). Foods should be in a single layer in the pan. The more items you fry the less oil you'll need and vice versa.

When is the oil ready? For deep frying, oil should reach about 375° on a deep-frying thermometer. To test it for readiness, put a piece of the food in it; if it sizzles and does not burn, proceed as specified in the recipe. Otherwise, raise or reduce the heat accordingly.

Small, delicate ingredients like nuts, "cellophane" noodles, shrimp chips, and *wonton* skins (see **Snacks: Sweet and**

Savory) cook very quickly; they must be watched carefully and scooped out at the right moment lest they burn. More solid foods, such as meatballs and potatoes in batter, pose no such problem.

Deep-fried foods should be crisp on the outside and tender and soft on the inside. If you wish to get a nice, golden brown color, use half fresh and half used oil. To recycle oil, cool it to room temperature and strain to remove any solid particles. Leave it in an open container so that undesirable odors will escape. To refresh the oil, add a chunk of dry ginger while heating it; leave for 30 seconds and then remove and discard it before adding the food. Use all-purpose vegetable oils for deep frying: peanut, corn, soybean, or cottonseed oil.

Don't be afraid of deep frying—learn, enjoy, and do it!

Quick-Fried Romaine Lettuce *Until now you probably have only eaten Romaine or Cos lettuce in a salad. But these tender leaves are cooked and eaten hot in Taiwan. Surprise your guests with this "Oriental" dish.*

1 to 1¼ pounds
  Romaine or Cos
  lettuce
¼ cup oil
½ teaspoon salt
½ teaspoon sugar

PREPARATION: 3 minutes
COOKING: 3 minutes
UTENSILS: colander or paper towels
3-quart saucepan with lid
long-handled spoon

STEPS

1. Trim root end of lettuce and remove tough outer leaves and discard. Wash remaining lettuce, shake off excess water, and drain well or pat dry. Cut into 1½-inch pieces.
2. Heat saucepan, then oil. Add lettuce, cover immediately, and shake pan over high heat until the sizzling stops. Remove cover and stir for 1 minute. Sprinkle salt and sugar over the lettuce and mix for 2 minutes more until the leaves become soft and wilted, but not brown. Serve hot.

Quick-Fried *Bok Choy*
Three of the simplest ingredients result in a superb Chinese cabbage dish. Duck fat gives the cabbage a distinctive rich taste and glossy sheen.

1 to 1¼ pounds *bok choy*
3 tablespoons duck or chicken fat, or ¼ cup oil
½ teaspoon salt

PREPARATION: 3 minutes
COOKING: 3 minutes
UTENSILS: colander
3-quart saucepan with lid
long-handled spoon

STEPS

1. Trim root end of *bok choy*. Wash and dry well. At a 45° slant, cut the stalks and leaves into 1½-inch pieces.
2. Heat saucepan, then oil. Add vegetables, cover immediately, and shake pan over heat briefly until sizzling stops. Remove lid and mix vegetables for 1 minute. Sprinkle salt over the *bok choy* and mix for 2 minutes more. Serve hot.

Cooking with Oil   95

Quick-Fried Bean Sprouts
Bean sprouts cooked simply, seasoned simply, and served simply are a true home-style delight—sweet and crunchy. Cook them quickly to preserve these qualities.

¾ to 1 pound fresh
   bean sprouts
¼ cup oil
2   scallions, finely
   sliced
½ teaspoon red or
   white vinegar
½ teaspoon salt

PREPARATION: 2 minutes
   COOKING: 2 to 3 minutes
   UTENSILS: colander
              10-inch skillet with lid
              long-handled spoon

STEPS

1. Wash bean sprouts and drain in colander until quite dry (up to 1 hour ahead if possible).
2. Heat skillet, then oil. Add bean sprouts and scallions, cover immediately, and shake skillet over high heat until the sizzling stops. Remove cover, add vinegar and salt, and mix for 1 or 2 minutes more. Serve hot.

TIP

The small amount of vinegar makes the bean sprouts crispier.

Chinese Leek Omelet
Chinese leeks look like a cross between scallions and chives. They are usually sold in Chinese markets or street stalls in fist-size bunches by weight. They are about 12 inches long and only ¼ to ⅜ inch wide. They have a delicate pungency that livens up this omelet.

4 **large or 5 small eggs, well beaten**
1 **teaspoon oil**
 ¼ **teaspoon salt**
 ½ **cup Chinese leeks or scallion greens, minced**
3 **tablespoons oil**

PREPARATION: 5 minutes
COOKING: 5 minutes
UTENSILS: mixing bowl
10-inch skillet
fork or chopsticks
spatula

STEPS

1. Beat eggs, add 1 teaspoon oil and the salt, and mix well.
2. Wash leeks and cut off and discard white root ends. Combine eggs and leeks and mix well.
3. Heat skillet and then oil; reduce heat to medium or medium-low. Pour in egg and leek mixture so that you swirl it evenly over the bottom of the skillet. Cook on *one side only*; tilt the pan so the softer egg mixture slides to the edges to cook and becomes firm (about 4 to 5 minutes). Use spatula to turn omelet out onto plate, with its browned, crispy side up. Serve hot.

VARIATION

For added taste and color add 2 tablespoons fresh or canned mushrooms, minced, to the egg-leek mixture.

Quick-Fried Pork and Preserved Cucumbers

½ pound pork loin
3 tablespoons oil
1 small onion
1 cup preserved cucumbers, canned, shredded

MARINADE
1 tablespoon water
½ tablespoon cornstarch
½ tablespoon sherry
¼ teaspoon sugar

PREPARATION: 10 minutes
MARINATING: 10 minutes
COOKING: 7 minutes
UTENSILS: 3-quart saucepan with lid
small bowl
slotted spoon

STEPS
1. Cut pork and onions into 2 × ¼-inch pieces.
2. Mix marinade ingredients well and combine with pork. Marinate for 10 minutes.
3. Heat saucepan, then oil. Add pork, quickly cover pan, and shake over heat for 1 minute. Remove lid and stir 3 to 4 minutes until all traces of pink are gone.
4. Add onions and preserved cucumbers and stir for 2 minutes more. Serve hot.

String Beans, Taiwan Style *These string beans are a snap to make. Quickly cooked with two sauces—one savory, the other sweet—they will turn out nice and crunchy.*

PREPARATION: 10 minutes
COOKING: 5 minutes
UTENSILS: 3-quart saucepan with lid
long-handled spoon
two small bowls

1	**pound fresh string beans**
3	**tablespoons oil**

SAUCE A
2	**tablespoons water**
1	**teaspoon soy sauce**
¼	**teaspoon salt**

SAUCE B
2	**tablespoons water**
1	**teaspoon soy sauce**
1	**teaspoon sugar**

STEPS

1. Snap off the ends of the beans, then bend them so they break into 1½-inch pieces. Wash and drain well.

2. Combine the sauce ingredients, keeping each sauce separate.

3. Heat saucepan, then oil. Add string beans; mix and stir for 2 minutes. Add Sauce A and cover pan immediately; cook for 2 minutes over medium heat. Add Sauce B and mix. Serve hot.

TIP

Do not be concerned if the beans look shrivelled and brown in spots; such an appearance is expected from this recipe. Do not overcook them.

 GOOD FOR BEGINNERS

Quick-Fried White Cabbage

and Ham *Ham and cabbage, Chinese style, is a fine last minute dish for lunch or a family-style dinner; it's quite simple and very good.*

1	**to 1½ pounds white cabbage**
¼	**pound cooked boiled ham**
¼	**cup oil or duck fat**
1	**teaspoon salt**
1	**cup water**

PREPARATION: 5 minutes
COOKING: 7 minutes
UTENSILS: 3-quart saucepan with lid
long-handled spoon

STEPS

1. Remove tough outer leaves and discard. Cut cabbage in half and remove the hard white core. Shred cabbage across into 2 × ⅜-inch pieces. Cut ham into same-size slices.

2. Heat saucepan, then oil. Add cabbage, cover immediately, and shake pan over high heat for 2 minutes. Remove lid, add salt, and stir; add water and stir for about 3 minutes. Add ham to pan and stir for 1 or 2 minutes. Serve hot.

TIP

A small cabbage is more tender and may not have a hard white core.

Quick-Fried Pork with Snow Peas

5   dried Chinese mushrooms
2   tablespoons mushroom soaking liquid or water
½ pound pork butt or thin, boned pork chops
¼ pound fresh or frozen snow peas
3   tablespoons oil
1   clove garlic, minced
½ teaspoon salt

MARINADE

1   teaspoon soy sauce
1   teaspoon sherry
1   teaspoon cornstarch

PREPARATION: 20 minutes
SOAKING: 20 minutes
MARINATING: 10 minutes
COOKING: 7 minutes
UTENSILS: 2 bowls
3-quart saucepan with lid
long-handled spoon

STEPS

1. Soak mushrooms in hot water, covered, for 20 minutes. Cut off and discard stems and leave caps whole. Reserve soaking liquid.
2. Wash snow peas. Snap off the tips, remove the stems and strings, and dry thoroughly.
3. Cut pork across the grain (to increase tenderness) into 2 × 1 × ¼-inch pieces (about the same size as the snow peas).
4. Mix marinade ingredients well and combine with pork slices. Marinate for 10 minutes.
5. Heat saucepan, then oil. Add garlic, pork, and mushrooms; stir and mix. Cover, reduce heat to medium, and let pork cook until all traces of pink are gone and it turns light brown. Add snow peas and stir; then add water or mushroom soaking liquid and salt. Stir for 1 minute. Serve hot.

TIPS

Snow peas are flat, pale green Chinese garden peas with pods, about 2 to 4 inches long, ¾ inch wide, and only ⅛ inch thick. When cooked they turn bright green and have a crunchy texture; they can be eaten pod and all! They will be least expensive during the summer months.

Snow peas smaller than 2 inches probably will not need to be destringed. However, frozen snow peas, even when thawed, should be destringed. Be sure to pat dry thoroughly.

Beef with Onions in Hoisin Sauce

Tender steak slices and tart onions are transformed when combined with sweet hoisin sauce.

½ **pound flank steak**
1 **medium onion**
¼ **cup oil**
1 **tablespoon oil**
2 **tablespoons hoisin
   sauce**

MARINADE
½ **tablespoon sherry**
¼ **teaspoon salt**
1 **clove garlic,
   minced**

PREPARATION: 10 minutes
MARINATING: 10 minutes
COOKING: 3 minutes
UTENSILS: small bowl
3-quart saucepan with lid
long-handled spoon

STEPS

1. Cut flank steak across the grain into 2 × ½ × ¼-inch pieces.
2. Mix marinade ingredients well and combine with steak slices. Marinate for 10 minutes.
3. Cut onion into 1½ × 1 × ¼-inch pieces.
4. Heat saucepan, then ¼ cup oil. Slide in beef with pan lid, cover immediately, and shake over heat until sizzling stops. Remove beef and set aside.
5. Add 1 tablespoon oil, then onions; stir for 1 minute. Add hoisin sauce and stir for 1 minute. Add beef; stir and mix for a few seconds. Serve hot with Steamed Buns (p. 42). Put mouthfuls of food into each bun and eat like a tiny sandwich.

Quick-Fried Broccoli

¾ to 1 pound broccoli
  florets
¼ cup oil
2 teaspoons salt
¼ cup water

OPTIONAL
5 dried Chinese
  mushroom caps,
  already soaked

SUBSTITUTE
Use cauliflower
florets instead of
broccoli florets.

PREPARATION: 15 minutes
  COOKING: 5 minutes
  UTENSILS: 10-inch skillet with cover
    small knife
    long-handled spoon

STEPS

1. Cut off most of the thick broccoli stems and use them to make Salted Broccoli Stems (p. 83). Peel the remaining stems by making a small cut in the bottom of each stem and slowly pulling up about ⅛ inch of the tougher outer skin to expose the tender, whitish green flesh. Trim knobs and dark green leaves and discard.

2. Wash florets and drain well (up to an hour ahead if possible).

3. Heat saucepan, then oil. Slide broccoli into pan, cover, and immediately shake over heat for 10 seconds. Remove lid, add salt, and stir; add water, and stir in a circular motion for 3 to 4 minutes until broccoli turns bright green. Serve hot.

Quick-Fried Snow Peas, Pressed Bean Curd, and Dried Mushrooms

Colors and textures abound in this vegetarian dish. Crunchy, jade-green snow peas, smooth, tan pressed bean curd, and chewy, lacquer-black mushrooms all glisten appetizingly with oil.

6 dried Chinese mushrooms
2 tablespoons mushroom soaking liquid or water
¼ pound fresh snow peas
2 squares flavored pressed bean curd
¼ cup oil
4 slices ginger
1 teaspoon salt

PREPARATION: 10 minutes
SOAKING: 20 minutes
COOKING: 3 minutes
UTENSILS: small bowl
3-quart saucepan
long-handled spoon

STEPS

1. Soak mushrooms in hot water, covered, for 20 minutes. Cut off and discard stems and cut caps in half. Reserve soaking liquid.
2. Wash snow peas. Snap off the tips, remove the stems and strings, and dry thoroughly.
3. Cut bean curd squares into ¼-inch slices.
4. Heat saucepan, then oil. Add ginger, mushrooms, and snow peas; stir and mix for 1 minute. Remove lid and *quickly* add salt and mushroom liquid (or water).
5. Add the bean curd and stir for 1 minute. Remove ginger. Serve hot.

Pork with Eggs and "Cloud Ears"

This well-known Northern favorite is often served inside thin Mandarin pancakes; they are rolled around the filling and tucked up at the ends to keep the juices from dripping out.

¼ cup dried "cloud
   ears"
¾ pound pork butt
¼ cup oil
2 eggs, lightly beaten
3 tablespoons oil
1 tablespoon garlic,
   finely sliced
2 scallions, in 1-inch
   pieces

MARINADE
1 tablespoon soy
   sauce
1 tablespoon sherry
1 tablespoon
   cornstarch
¼ teaspoon salt

PREPARATION: 10 minutes
SOAKING: 10 minutes
MARINATING: 10 minutes
COOKING: 10 minutes
UTENSILS: small bowls
        3-quart saucepan with lid
        long-handled spoon

STEPS

1. Soak "cloud ears" in boiling water, covered, for 10 minutes. Drain and rinse well to remove dirt particles. If the "cloud ears" are very large, cut them into 1-inch squares.
2. Cut pork across the grain into $1 \times \frac{1}{2} \times \frac{1}{4}$-inch pieces.
3. Mix marinade ingredients well and combine with pork slices. Marinate for 10 minutes.
4. Heat saucepan, then ¼ cup oil. Pour in eggs, cook for 1 minute, then stir until egg mixture is firm. Transfer to dish and set aside.
5. Heat 3 tablespoons oil. Add pork and garlic and stir for 4 to 5 minutes until the pork loses all traces of pink and turns light brown. Add "cloud ears"; stir a few times. Add eggs, stir, and turn heat off. Add scallions and mix. Serve hot, with or without Mandarin Pancakes (see **Store-to-Table: The Chinese Grocery,** p. 149).

Quick-Fried Eggplant *Black beans and garlic are a common accompaniment to eggplant.*

1 **large or 6 baby eggplants (about 1½ pounds)**
5 **tablespoons oil**
3 **tablespoons fermented black beans, minced**
1 **tablespoon garlic, minced**
⅔ **cup water**
1 **teaspoon salt**
½ **teaspoon sugar**

OPTIONAL
4 **dried Chinese mushroom caps, shredded**
¼ **pound ground pork**

PREPARATION: 10 minutes
COOKING: 10 minutes
UTENSILS: 4-quart saucepan with lid
long-handled spoon

STEPS

1. Wash the eggplant and trim the knobby stem if you use a large one. Cut large eggplants into quarters, lengthwise. (Cut small eggplants in half, lengthwise.) Then cut strips across into ⅜-inch pieces.

2. Heat saucepan, then oil. Add black beans and garlic. Stir for 1 to 2 minutes until garlic turns brown and odor of beans is released.

3. Reduce heat to medium. Add eggplant pieces, a handful at a time, and mix for 2 minutes. Add water, cover, and simmer for 5 minutes; stir twice. Add salt and sugar and mix once more. Serve hot or at room temperature.

TIPS

Cut eggplant just before cooking so it won't discolor.

If you use the optional ingredients, add them after **Step 2**; stir for a few minutes until the pork loses all traces of pink and turns light brown.

Beef with Pickled String Beans

½ pound flank steak
¼ pound pickled
  string beans (p. 84)
¼ cup oil
  salt

MARINADE
1 teaspoon sherry
¼ teaspoon salt
4 cloves garlic,
   minced

PREPARATION: 5 minutes
MARINATING: 10 minutes
COOKING: 5 minutes
UTENSILS: small bowl
          3-quart saucepan with lid
          long-handled spoon

STEPS

1. Cut flank steak across the grain into $2 \times 1 \times$ ⅜-inch pieces.
2. Mix marinade ingredients well and combine with steak slices. Marinate for 10 minutes.
3. Cut each string bean into shreds, lengthwise.
4. Heat saucepan, then oil. Slide in beef with pan lid, cover immediately, and shake over heat until sizzling stops. Remove lid and stir for 1 to 2 minutes. Remove beef and set aside.
5. Add string beans and stir for 2 minutes. Return beef; stir and mix for 30 seconds. Add salt to taste. Serve hot.

Deep-Fried Meatballs

These tasty meatballs are excellent for appetizers, family meals, buffets, and picnics. They are enhanced with a sweet plum sauce dip and a spicy pepper dip.

2 cups oil

MEATBALL MIXTURE
½ pound ground lean pork
½ pound ground lean beef
1 egg, well beaten
1 tablespoon water
1 teaspoon sherry
1½ tablespoons cornstarch
½ tablespoon salt
½ tablespoon sugar

SWEET DIP
¼ cup canned Plum Sauce

SPICY DIP
½ tablespoon ground black pepper

PREPARATION: 15 minutes
COOKING: 5 to 8 minutes
YIELD: 20 meatballs
UTENSILS: fork
mixing bowl
3 to 4-quart saucepan
slotted spoon
paper towels

STEPS

1. With a fork or your fingers thoroughly combine the ingredients for the meatballs in a mixing bowl. To make each meatball, firmly press, then roll about 1 tablespoon of the mixture into a ball between your palms. Repeat until you use up all the meat (about 20 meatballs).
2. Heat oil for about 5 minutes. Reduce heat to medium and add meatballs (they will sizzle); cook 5 to 8 minutes or until they are brown on the outside. Remove them from the oil and drain on paper towels. Serve hot or at room temperature with little dishes of plum sauce and black pepper.

TIPS

A beef and pork combination provides a harmonious blend of tender and fatty meats, but you may use either one or the other.

Allow the meatballs to cool for a couple of minutes before biting into them—the insides will be piping hot and you may burn your tongue!

These meatballs make excellent hors d'oeuvres. Spear a toothpick in each meatball and place on a plate with a dip in the center.

Batter-Fried Potatoes

1 to 1¼ pounds all-
purpose potatoes
2 cups oil

BATTER
1 egg
3 tablespoons flour
2 tablespoons water
1½ tablespoons sugar
¼ teaspoon baking
powder

PREPARATION: 10 minutes
COOKING: 10 minutes
UTENSILS: mixing bowl
peeler
3-quart saucepan
long-handled spoon
paper towels

STEPS

1. Combine batter ingredients and mix thoroughly. Peel potatoes and cut into ⅜-inch rounds and then into ½-inch-wide sticks. Put half of the potatoes into the batter and coat well.
2. Heat saucepan, then oil (use medium heat). When oil is ready, shake excess batter off potatoes and add them piece by piece to pan. Deep fry 2 minutes only; turn them over and cook 1 minute more until they are golden brown outside and tender inside. Coat the remaining potatoes with the batter and deep fry as above. Drain on paper towels. Serve hot.

VARIATION

Use ½ pound sweet potatoes. Choose long, evenly rounded ones. Trim the ends and leave the skin on. Scrub them well and remove any root hairs. Add ¼ teaspoon salt to the batter and cook as above.

TIPS

Let potatoes cool off a couple of minutes before biting into them so you won't burn your tongue.

These make healthy, after-school snacks for children.

"Cellophane" Noodles with Meat Sauce, Szechuan Style

Deep-fried "cellophane" noodles turn into light, airy puffs of white that look like birds' nests. They complement a celestial sauce pungently seasoned and spiced.

3 cups oil
2 ounces "cellophane" noodles

MEAT SAUCE
¼ cup oil
1 tablespoon garlic, minced
¼ cup scallions, finely sliced
2 tablespoons hoisin sauce
1 tablespoon soy sauce
½ cup bamboo shoots, minced
¼ cup Szechuan mustard pickle, minced
6 ounces ground beef
1 tablespoon cornstarch
1 cup water

PREPARATION: 25 minutes
COOKING: 10 minutes
UTENSILS: large plate
kitchen shears or scissors
2 3-quart saucepans
strainer
paper towels
long-handled spoon
serving platter

STEPS

1. Over a large plate, pull apart and partially separate the noodles so they'll expand and puff up nicely when deep fried. Using kitchen shears or scissors, cut them into three batches.
2. Preheat oven to 250°.
3. To make meat sauce, heat ¼ cup oil. Add garlic and scallions and stir for 30 seconds. Add hoisin sauce and soy sauce and stir. Add bamboo shoots, Szechuan mustard pickle, and beef. Mix and stir. Combine cornstarch and water and add to pan. Bring to a boil. Cook and stir for 5 minutes.
4. Heat 3 cups of oil. Test for readiness by putting a small piece of noodle into the oil. It should rise to the surface and turn white. Deep fry one batch of noodles at a time and turn them over as soon as they rise to the surface (about 2 or 3 seconds). Drain on paper towels and repeat with the other batches. Remove paper towels and put noodles in oven to keep warm.
5. When ready to serve, arrange noodles on platter and ladle meat sauce on top. Serve hot.

"Four Happinesses" Meatball Casserole

In China this dish of four large meatballs, sandwiched between layers of Chinese cabbage, symbolizes happiness, joy, long life, and prosperity. It is an excellent, hearty, one-pot meal.

1 pound Chinese cabbage (Napa)
2 cups oil
½ cup Soy Sauce Stock (p. 4)
¼ cup water

MEATBALL MIXTURE
½ pound ground pork
½ pound ground beef
1 egg, well beaten
1 tablespoon water
1 tablespoon sherry
2 tablespoons cornstarch
2 tablespoons sugar
½ tablespoon salt

PREPARATION: 15 minutes
COOKING: 35 minutes
UTENSILS: mixing bowl
3-quart saucepan or 10-inch skillet
3-quart saucepan or casserole with lid
slotted spoon

STEPS

1. Trim root end of cabbage, separate leaves, and wash. Cut in half across the width and separate the thick white stems and pale green leaves into two piles.

2. Combine the Soy Sauce Stock and water and set aside.

3. With a fork or your fingers thoroughly combine the ingredients for the meatballs in a mixing bowl. Divide the mixture into four equal parts. To make each large meatball, firmly press, then roll each fourth of the mixture into a ball, 2½ to 3 inches in diameter, between your palms.

4. Heat oil in saucepan or skillet for about 5 minutes. Add meatballs, reduce heat to medium, and deep fry in bubbling oil 3 to 4 minutes until one side is brown. Gently turn meatballs over and cook another 3 to 4 minutes until brown. Remove from oil and set aside.

5. Line the bottom of the pan or casserole with the thick white stems and place the meatballs on top. Cover with the cabbage leaves. (If you can't fit all the leaves in the pan, wait a couple of minutes until they cook down and add the rest later.)

6. Pour the Soy Sauce Stock and water mixture on top and bring to a boil over moderate heat. Cover and simmer for 20 minutes. Serve hot.

To transform this dish into a soup, use a 4½-quart saucepan or casserole and add 2 cups of water in **Step 6.**

TIPS

You may use all beef or all pork for the meatballs rather than a combination of beef and pork.

If you have no Soy Sauce Stock on hand, use ¼ cup each of soy sauce, sherry, and water, plus ½ teaspoon sugar.

Soups:
Light and Hearty

Hot or chilled, soup is often a prelude to a Western lunch or supper and is then forgotten. The opposite is true in China. For the Chinese, soup is an essential, integral part of the menu. It appears along with the other courses and is the major liquid refreshment during a home-style midday or evening meal.

A large serving bowl of light or hearty soup is placed in the center of the table; it is surrounded by 4 dishes—beef or pork, chicken, vegetables, or seafood—along with rice, noodles or buns. To eat soup, Chinese style, the diner either dips his or her own spoon into the tureen or lifts an individual bowl, smaller than a rice bowl, to the mouth. The liquid is then sipped or sucked directly from the bowl, and the solid ingredients are picked up with chopsticks.

Chinese soups are preseasoned by the cook. Therefore it is not customary to add salt, pepper, or soy sauce at the table. Generally none of these condiments appears during a Chinese meal, unless as dips for bland foods, such as White-Cooked Chicken (p. 158), Boiled Spinach (p. 66), *Bok Choy* (p. 67), or Crispy Duck (p. 165).

Home-style soups usually have a light, thin stock as a base. Milk, cream, butter, and thickening agents that are common in Western soups and chowders are not used. Chinese soups can be delicate or robust, bland or spicy; they can be hot and sour and either made with familiar, inexpensive

Soups: Light and Hearty

homespun ingredients, or, for banquet dining, made with more exotic and costly items, such as special birds' nests or sharks' fins.

A light Bean Curd, "Cellophane" Noodle, or Watercress Soup, along with rice and 4 other courses, would make a fine summer meal. Heartier Meatball Soup or elegant Crabmeat and Chinese Cabbage Soup served with plain buns and perhaps one other course, would be more than adequate on a cold winter's day. Heavier Oxtail Soup and Steamed Buns would make a meal in themselves.

These soups are easy to prepare. They require no special utensils or cooking techniques, and will differ from any you may have eaten in Chinese restaurants. For the utmost enjoyment, be sure to serve soup hot. Bring it to the table garnished with minced, cooked ham or chopped Chinese parsley (cilantro). Or you can add drops of amber-colored sesame oil for extra flavor and sheen.

CHINESE SOUP STOCKS

A stock pot is almost always simmering in a Chinese kitchen. Bones and fatty meat scraps from pork and spareribs or chickens and ducks are tossed into it. Covered with plenty of water to which a chunk of ginger and a splash of wine have been added, these leftovers cook slowly and gently for hours, unattended, requiring only an occasional peek at the water level—a wonderful "cooking-without-the-cook" method. As the stock simmers, fat and impurities rise to the surface in the form of a foamy scum that should be skimmed until it is completely gone. This step takes only a minute and keeps the soup light and clear.

Stocks can also be by-products of other dishes. For example, Steamed Duck (p. 60) yields a rich duck stock, and White-Cooked Chicken (p. 158) provides a subtle chicken stock.

A good stock can make a world of difference, but if you don't have the time or the ingredients to make one yourself, canned chicken broth is an acceptable substitute with quite good results. (Beef broth is too strong.) The canned broth will be seasoned with salt and probably MSG (monosodium glutamate) and can be stretched with an equal amount of water. Home-cooked stock, on the other hand, should be salted to taste after cooking.

You will notice that the proportion of stock to water decreases as the flavor of the basic soup ingredients increases. Thus, bland bean curd simmers only in stock. Tasteless "cellophane" noodles require 4 cups of stock to 1 cup of water. Rich Meatball Soup needs only 1 cup of stock to 4 cups of water. At the other end of the scale, steer oxtails cook only in water; their meat enriches the liquid, while the gelatin in the bones adds body.

After cooling the stock to room temperature, refrigerate for 3 or 4 days. It can sour if left longer and must be boiled before using again. Stock can also be frozen up to 1 month in 1-pint plastic containers. Allow a 1-inch space at the top for the liquid to expand as it freezes. For this reason never use a glass jar. Stock takes a long time to thaw; to speed up the process put the container in a bowl of hot, running water.

Making your own stock from scratch is very satisfying, as the natural, good flavors it yields will enhance any soup. We also think it's a great way to fight inflation!

Pork Stock

1 **pound trimmings and bones from pork spareribs or raw pork chops**
2 **quarts cold water**
1 **chunk or 4 slices ginger**
1 **tablespoon sherry or Shao-Hsing rice wine**
½ **tablespoon salt**

PREPARATION: 5 minutes
COOKING: 2 to 4 hours
UTENSILS: 4-quart stewpot with lid
strainer

STEPS

1. Add ingredients to the pot and cover with water. Bring to a boil. Reduce heat to *very low,* cover, and gently simmer 2 to 4 hours. Skim scum. If necessary during the lengthy cooking time, add more boiling water to keep the ingredients covered.
2. Remove bones and fat. Strain liquid. Use for soups or cool to room temperature before storing in refrigerator 3 to 4 days.

TIPS

The longer you cook the stock, the more flavorful it will be. Increasing the amount of meat and bones also enriches the broth.

Skim fat before using. The stock can be frozen up to 1 month.

This recipe can easily be halved or doubled.

Bean Curd Soup *Pure and simple, this soup is the epitome of Chinese home-style cooking.*

2 bean curd squares
1 teaspoon salt
3 cups pork or chicken
stock
1 scallion, finely sliced
salt

OPTIONAL
sesame oil

PREPARATION: 5 minutes
SALTING: 10 minutes
COOKING: 10 minutes
UTENSILS: 2-quart saucepan with lid

STEPS

1. Cut bean curd into ½-inch cubes and sprinkle with the salt. Set aside for 10 minutes.
2. Bring stock to a boil, add bean curd cubes, and bring to boil again.
3. Stir in scallion slices, turn heat off, and immediately cover pan and let sit for 5 minutes.
4. Season with salt to taste. If you wish, float a couple of drops of sesame oil on top. Serve hot.

TIPS

Choose 3-inch squares of firm bean curd for the soup.

Covering the pot allows bland bean curd to more fully absorb the flavor of the stock.

Corn Soup
This attractive yellow soup with egg "flow-ers" floating in it and topped with minced ham looks and tastes delicious.

16 or 17-ounce can cream-style corn
1 cup chicken stock
2 cups water
2 eggs, well beaten
¼ teaspoon salt

OPTIONAL
1 slice cooked ham, minced
  sesame oil

PREPARATION: 5 minutes
COOKING: 7 minutes
UTENSILS: 3-quart saucepan
small bowl
slotted spoon

STEPS

1. Combine corn, stock, and water and bring to a boil, *uncovered*. Reduce heat to medium and simmer, uncovered, for 2 minutes.

2. *Slowly* pour well-beaten eggs through the openings of the slotted spoon into the saucepan. When the egg threads rise to the top, remove pan from heat, add salt, minced ham, and sesame oil. Serve hot.

TIPS

Pouring the eggs through the slotted spoon openings makes them come out in thin threads rather than thick globs.

This soup can be reheated nicely over moderate heat.

PREPARE AHEAD: 1 day

Duck Stock and Duck Fat
A good stock is a valuable commodity. This one is the effortless and economical by-product of Steamed Duck (p. 60) and can be used as a base for Duck Bone Soup (p. 123).

PREPARATION: see Steamed Duck
UTENSILS: bulb baster
strainer
heatproof 4-cup measuring cup or heatproof
1-quart bowl

STEPS

1. During the lengthy steaming process collect about 4 cups of pale brown liquid and golden yellow fat that seep together from the duck. Use a bulb baster and reserve liquid and fat in a heatproof container or bowl.

2. Strain out any solid particles and cool gradually to room temperature.

3. Refrigerate and cover securely. The stock will jell. The fat congeals into a solid, creamy-textured disk the color of sweet butter.

TIPS

Lift the fat up with a large spoon or spatula. Use it as a substitute for oil in Quick-Fried *Bok Choy* (p. 95), Quick-Fried White Cabbage and Ham (p. 99), Quick-Fried Romaine Lettuce (p. 94), or for Fried Rice and Onions in Duck Fat (p. 28).

You may leave the stock and fat in the refrigerator for several weeks or freeze them together or separately up to 1 month.

"Cellophane" Noodle Soup

Here is another delightful use for those translucent bean threads called "cellophane" noodles. Tasteless by themselves, they absorb the taste of the stock and add texture to the soup. They look pretty as well.

4 dried Chinese
  mushrooms
2 ounces "cellophane"
  noodles
4 cups pork, chicken,
  or duck stock
1 cup water
3 ounces Szechuan
  mustard pickle,
  shredded
1 tablespoon scallion
  greens, finely sliced

PREPARATION: 5 minutes
SOAKING: 20 minutes
COOKING: 15 minutes
UTENSILS: 2 small bowls
         2 to 3-quart saucepan with lid

STEPS

1. Soak dried Chinese mushrooms, covered, for 20 minutes. Drain, cut off and discard stems, and shred caps. Soak "cellophane" noodles in hot water for 10 minutes. Drain, cut in half, and set aside.

2. Combine stock, water, shredded mushrooms, and Szechuan mustard pickle in saucepan. Bring to a boil. Reduce heat to medium. Cook, covered, for 10 minutes.

3. Add noodles and scallions to stock, bring to boil again. Turn heat off. Serve immediately.

TIP

To reheat leftover soup, first scoop out the solid ingredients and then bring the stock to a boil. Turn heat off and return solid ingredients to pan; let soup sit and heat through for a couple of minutes before serving.

Duck Bone Soup

Chinese restaurants specializing in Peking Duck always use the carcasses and bones in a soothing duck bone and cabbage soup at the meal's end. You can make this surprisingly delicious and thrifty soup from leftover Crispy Duck (p. 165).

1 carcass left over from
  Crispy Duck
1 tablespoon duck fat
  from Steamed Duck
2 cups duck stock from
  Steamed Duck
4 cups water
1 pound Chinese
  cabbage (Napa)
  salt to taste

PREPARATION: 5 minutes
  COOKING: 25 minutes
  UTENSILS: 3½ to 5-quart stewpot or casserole with lid
        ladle

STEPS

1. Break the carcass into three pieces. Combine carcass, duck fat, duck stock, and water and bring to a boil.
2. Trim root end of cabbage and discard or use leftover leaves from Sweet "n" Sour Chinese Cabbage. Wash and cut *across* the fat part into 1½-inch pieces. Add cabbage to stewpot, mix, and bring to boil again. Cover, turn heat to *very low*, and cook for 15 minutes. Serve hot with pieces of carcass and bones; add salt to taste.

TIP
Pick meat from bones with your fingers or chopsticks.

Watercress Soup
Watercress and dried Chinese mushrooms are a favorite combination.

4   **dried Chinese mushrooms**
¼ to ½ **pound watercress**
3   **cups pork or chicken stock**
1   **cup water**
    salt

OPTIONAL
1   **slice cooked ham, shredded**
    sesame oil

PREPARATION: 5 minutes
SOAKING: 20 minutes
COOKING: 15 minutes
UTENSILS: small bowl
2-quart saucepan with lid

STEPS

1. Soak mushrooms in hot water, covered, for 20 minutes. Cut off and discard stems and slice caps into ¼-inch shreds.
2. Wash and drain watercress, cut into 2-inch pieces, and discard any tough stems.
3. Combine mushrooms, stock, and water and bring to a boil. Reduce heat to medium and simmer for 10 minutes. Add watercress and ham to saucepan and simmer for 5 minutes. Stir.
4. Season with salt to taste and add sesame oil if desired. Serve hot.

TIP

For a formal banquet add shredded cooked ham and put a small bottle of sesame oil on the table for individual seasoning.

Pork and Szechuan Mustard Pickle Soup
You will like this unusual soup made with China's favorite meat.

½ **pound pork butt**
¼ **pound Szechuan**
   mustard pickle
2 **cups chicken stock**
2 **cups water**
   sesame oil

MARINADE
1 **tablespoon sherry**
1 **teaspoon**
   cornstarch

PREPARATION: 10 minutes
MARINATING: 10 minutes
COOKING: 15 minutes
UTENSILS: small bowl
          2-quart saucepan with lid

STEPS

1. Cut pork into 1½ × ¼-inch shreds. Combine with marinade ingredients. Mix well and set aside for 10 minutes.
2. Cut Szechuan mustard pickle into 1½ × ¼-inch shreds. Combine mustard pickle, stock, and water and bring to a boil. Add pork, stir, cover pan, and cook over moderate heat for 10 minutes. Trickle sesame oil on top and serve hot.

TIP
Rinse the mustard pickle in cold water if you like it less spicy.

Winter Melon Soup

Winter melon is available year-round in Chinese groceries. Although the thought of putting melon in soup may sound odd, this melon imparts a special flavor to the soup that is at once delicate, unusual, and unforgettably delicious.

6   dried Chinese
    mushrooms
1   to 1½ pounds
    winter melon
1   cup chicken stock
3   cups water
4   slices ginger
½   tablespoon salt

OPTIONAL
1   slice cooked ham,
    shredded
    sesame oil

PREPARATION: 5 minutes
    SOAKING: 20 minutes
    COOKING: 20 minutes
    UTENSILS: small bowl with cover
              3-quart saucepan with lid

STEPS

1. Soak mushrooms in hot water, covered, for 20 minutes. Cut off and discard stems and leave caps whole.

2. Scoop out and discard the yellow seeds and spongy section of the melon. Trim the dark green rind and cut firm melon flesh into 1½-inch chunks. Slice each chunk into ⅜-inch pieces.

3. Add all main ingredients to the saucepan, bring to a boil, reduce heat to medium, and simmer, covered, for 15 minutes. If desired, add the shredded ham and sesame oil at the last minute. Serve hot.

TIPS

Huge winter melons are sold by the slice in Chinese groceries. The exposed flesh should be firm and crispy white with no brown spots. The price will naturally be lower during the winter months.

While it is best to use melon right away, it can be stored in the refrigerator for 3 or 4 days with a piece of wax paper folded over the flesh.

Crabmeat and Chinese Cabbage

Soup *Here we offer a more sophisticated dish using basic Chinese ingredients—fresh, canned, and dried—that accent the crabmeat without masking its sweetness.*

2 ounces "cellophane" noodles
4 dried Chinese mushrooms
½ cup bamboo shoots
1 to 1½ pounds Chinese cabbage (Napa)
6 to 8 ounces crabmeat (canned, fresh, or frozen)
2 pieces ginger
1½ cups mushroom soaking liquid or water
½ tablespoon sherry
½ teaspoon salt

PREPARATION: 15 minutes
SOAKING: 20 minutes
COOKING: 25 minutes
UTENSILS: small bowls
colander
3-quart saucepan or casserole with lid

STEPS

1. Soak "cellophane" noodles in warm water for 20 minutes. Drain and cut in half. Soak dried mushrooms in hot water, covered, for 20 minutes (reserve the mushroom soaking liquid). Cut off and discard stems and leave caps whole. Cut bamboo shoots into 2 × ¼-inch pieces.

2. Trim root end of cabbage, separate leaves, and wash. Cut the heart into quarters and the stems and leaves into 2-inch pieces. Line the bottom of the saucepan or casserole with the thick white stems. Reserve the leaves.

3. Put the crabmeat on top of the cabbage and spread it around. Add the mushrooms, bamboo shoots, and ginger slices; place the remaining cabbage on top.

4. Combine the mushroom soaking liquid or water, the sherry, and the salt and pour into pan. Cover and bring to a boil. Reduce heat to *medium low* and simmer, covered, for 20 minutes. Add "cellophane" noodles and push them under the liquid. Cover and cook 5 minutes. Serve hot.

Meatball Soup
This marvelous soup features delicate meatballs and smooth Chinese cabbage in a broth that is subtly flavored with ginger.

1 to 1½ pounds Chinese cabbage (Napa)
1 cup pork or chicken stock
4 cups water
4 slices ginger
   ½ tablespoon salt

MEATBALL MIXTURE
¼ pound lean ground beef
½ tablespoon cornstarch
½ tablespoon sherry
½ tablespoon water
½ teaspoon salt
⅛ teaspoon sugar

PREPARATION: 15 minutes
COOKING: 20 minutes
UTENSILS: 3-quart saucepan with lid
mixing bowl
fork

STEPS

1. Trim root end of cabbage and discard; or use leftover leaves from Sweet "n" Sour Chinese Cabbage. Cut cabbage into 1 × 1½-inch pieces and rinse.

2. Combine the cabbage, stock, and water and turn heat to high. Add ginger and salt; stir and wait a couple of minutes for the cabbage to cook down. Cover and cook about 7 minutes until the soup comes to a rapid boil.

3. With a fork or your fingers thoroughly combine the ingredients for the meatballs in a mixing bowl. To make each meatball, firmly press, then roll about ½ tablespoon of the mixture into a ball between your palms. Repeat until you use up all the meat (about 15 meatballs). Add meatballs to the soup and cover; turn heat to medium and cook for 10 minutes. Serve hot.

TIP

To reheat leftover soup, add an extra cup of water and salt to taste.

PREPARE AHEAD: The meatballs can be made several hours before and kept in the refrigerator. Warm them to room temperature before cooking.

Oxtail Soup

This recipe makes enough soup for several people—perhaps a family-style meal or a midwinter luncheon. The broth is silky, the vegetables soft, and the meat around the bones succulent.

1½ pounds oxtail in 1½ to 2-inch pieces
2 medium onions
2 large all-purpose potatoes
2 tomatoes
2 tablespoons sherry
2 tablespoons salt

OPTIONAL
2 carrots

PREPARATION: 15 minutes
COOKING: 2 hours 15 minutes
UTENSILS: 4 to 5-quart stewpot or casserole with lid
ladle

STEPS

1. Wash oxtail pieces.
2. Peel and cut each onion into 6 wedges. Peel and cut carrots into ½-inch pieces. Peel and cut potatoes into ½-inch cubes. Cut each tomato into 6 wedges.
3. Combine meat, onions, sherry, and salt and cover with water to within 1 inch of the rim. Bring to a boil. Reduce heat to medium. Cover, leaving lid ajar about ½ inch. Simmer for 1 hour.
4. Check water level. If it has boiled down, add 2 cups *boiling* water, partially cover again, and simmer for ½ hour more.
5. Add potatoes, tomatoes, and carrots to soup. If necessary, add more boiling water to keep water level within 1 inch of the rim. Cover and simmer for final ½ hour. Serve hot.

TIP

You may lay a bamboo chopstick across the outer edge of the rim of the pot or casserole and put the lid on top of it instead of leaving the lid partially ajar.

PREPARE AHEAD: 1 day; Oxtail Soup tastes even better the second day.

Snacks:
Sweet and Savory

Snacks, sweet and savory, play an important and beloved part of Chinese life for old and young. No excuse is needed to eat them from midmorning until midnight. They are enjoyed as a break at work, after school, during a late night game of *mahjong*, or nibbled with tea or wine. Whether homemade, bought in specialty shops, at bakeries, or from itinerant vendors, their variety is quite amazing and imaginative. Yet they are easy to duplicate in your own kitchen.

Delight your guests at a game of cards with sweet chilled Almond Junket or hot, fruit-laden December 8 Festival Rice. Surprise the children with Baked Pork or Bean Paste Buns while they are doing their homework. Or, munch on Deep-Fried Sugared Walnuts or Salted Peanuts while reading or watching television. All are delicious, nutritious, and pleasantly filling snacks.

Some snacks are fun to make. For example, family members can join in preparing Crispy Twists or fashioning batches of *wontons* (p. 38) for "soup" or deep frying. Even fixing meat buns and sweet buns is an enjoyable pastime.

Savory snacks can also serve as light meals: a large bowl of *Wonton* "Soup" (p. 39) with leftover meat and vegetables; Chinese sausages and raw leeks; Steamed New Potatoes (p. 58); Tea Leaf Eggs; Steamed Beef Buns.

It has always been a custom among Chinese families to exchange presents of food when visiting someone's home, especially during their New Year. Snacks, such as ours, make an ideal gift any time.

Snacks: Sweet and Savory

Almond Junket
This delicious almond-flavored junket, smooth and white as snow with crushed ice floating on it, is instantly cooling; it is enjoyed as a summertime snack in China and is eaten plain or fancy with colorful fruits.

1 cup water
1 envelope or 1 tablespoon unflavored gelatin
2 tablespoons granulated sugar
1 cup whole or lowfat milk
1 tablespoon almond extract
crushed ice
sugar

OPTIONAL
chilled 11-ounce can of fruit cocktail; canned lichees, loquats, or mandarin orange segments

PREPARATION: 5 minutes
CHILLING: 2 hours or overnight
UTENSILS: 1-quart saucepan with lid
bread loaf or square pan
wooden spoon
knife or spatula

STEPS

1. Bring water to a boil. Pour the gelatin and 2 tablespoons sugar into the loaf or square pan. Simultaneously add the boiling water and stir the mixture for 1 minute until the gelatin and sugar are *completely dissolved.* Add milk and almond extract and stir.

2. Put the pan in the refrigerator until the junket sets (in 2 hours or overnight). Slide a knife or spatula around the sides of the junket to separate it from the pan; then neatly cut the junket into 1-inch cubes or diamonds. Carefully loosen and slide about 4 pieces per bowl into individual bowls. To each bowl add 2 tablespoons crushed ice or ice water and 1 teaspoon sugar. Mix well, but gently. Serve cold, with or without fruits.

TIPS
Do not use skim milk.

Make individual molds by pouring the hot mixture into small bowls and then cutting the junket just before serving.

Before adding chilled fruits drain the syrup and pile the fruits on top of the junket; add crushed ice but omit the sugar.

PREPARE AHEAD: 1 day

December 8 Festival Rice

December 8

Festival Rice is served in North China when preparations for the Chinese New Year begin. On the lunar calendar New Year's day usually falls between late January and the middle of February. An Oriental cousin of our Christmas fruit cake, Festival Rice is a thick, sweet porridge of glazed or dried fruits, nuts, seeds, beans, and grains mingled with glutinous rice instead of dough.

Traditionally, the making of Festival Rice reminded the Chinese housekeeper that it was time to check out her storage room as part of the overall cleaning required for the New Year. She would take an inventory of the ingredients that went into the richly laden rice and prepare a shopping list of supplies needed for the coming months.

When served as a late afternoon or midnight refreshment, a bowlful of hot December 8 Festival Rice warmed one's insides and previewed weeks of feasting ahead. The rice, grains, fruits, and nuts it contained symbolized hope for a prosperous year.

PREPARATION: 15 minutes
SOAKING: 3 to 8 hours
COOKING: 1 hour 10 minutes
UTENSILS: bowl
colander
4-quart saucepan with lid
wooden spoon

¾ cup glutinous rice
2 quarts water
½ cup glazed fruits
(fruit cake mix) or
½ cup dried fruits
(apples, apricots,
pears, pineapple,
raisins)
½ cup shelled walnuts
¼ cup roasted
peanuts
⅓ cup white or brown
sugar
1 tablespoon wheat
germ or cornmeal
½ teaspoon white
sesame seeds

SUBSTITUTE
**Instead of wheat
germ or cornmeal
you may use
uncooked Cream of
Wheat or
Wheatena cereal.**

STEPS

1. Soak the rice in cold water for 3 to 8 hours. Drain, add to saucepan, and cover with water. Bring to a boil.
2. Reduce the heat to medium and cook, covered, for 1 hour. Check to make sure the rice doesn't boil over.
3. While stirring constantly, add all the other ingredients; continue stirring over moderate heat for 10 minutes. Serve in individual bowls with a spoon for each person. Serve hot or at room temperature.

TIP

Store leftover porridge in the refrigerator up to 3 days. To reheat add water.

Baked Bean Paste Buns *Baked or steamed buns with all kinds of fillings, sweet and savory, are a favorite snack throughout China. As a substitute for rolling your own dough we recommend plain, oven-ready refrigerated biscuits in a tube. These are handy, inexpensive, and save time. By combining tradition with convenience and getting worthwhile results, you will be encouraged to make buns more often.*

PREPARATION: 20 minutes
COOKING: 10 minutes
UTENSILS: rolling pin or tall glass
baking sheet
YIELD: 10 buns

½ cup sweetened red
   bean paste
10 plain oven-ready
   biscuits
1 tablespoon all-
   purpose flour

OPTIONAL
2 teaspoons white or
   black sesame seeds

STEPS

1. Roll 1 teaspoon of bean paste into a round ball and repeat until there are 10. Set them aside.

2. Preheat oven to 450° or the temperature listed on the tube of biscuits.

3. Separate the biscuits and dust both sides lightly with flour. Roll a biscuit into a 3-inch round. Hold it in one hand which is slightly cupped, and put the bean paste ball in its center. With the thumb and index finger of the other hand carefully but quickly pinch and pleat the edges together. Keep turning the bun slightly until the pleats meet and swirl in the center and completely cover the filling. Repeat until you have 10 round buns.

4. Gently flatten each bun with the palm of your hand until it is about 2 inches across. Press the pleated side into the sesame seeds and shake off any excess seeds. Repeat with all the buns and immediately place them, sesame seed or pleated-side up, on a baking sheet, ½ inch apart. Bake for 10 minutes or until brown on top. Serve hot.

TIPS

These buns require practice and patience to perfect. Work quickly so the dough doesn't shrink.

Buns taste best when fresh, but can be stored in a tightly sealed plastic container in the refrigerator up to 4 days. To reheat, put them in a 350° oven for 5 to 8 minutes.

Be careful biting into the buns, for the filling is hot enough to burn. Let them cool first for a couple of minutes.

Crispy Twists

These pretty twists sprinkled with confectioners' sugar are children's favorites. Chinese families give them as gifts during their New Year and keep a supply on hand for visitors.

12 wonton skins
3 cups oil
2 tablespoons confectioners' sugar

PREPARATION: 10 minutes
COOKING: 5 to 8 minutes
UTENSILS: 3-quart saucepan
slotted spoon
sifter
paper towels
YIELD: 12 crispy twists

STEPS

1. Stack the *wonton* skins and cut them in half by pressing a sharp knife firmly down through their middles. To make each *wonton* twist put two halves together, one on top of the other. Carefully cut 3 slits in the center; they should be 2 inches long and separated from each other and the edges by ⅜ inch. Hold one end of the skins and put your other thumb and index finger through the middle slit. Pull the other end of the two skins *up through it*. Repeat with remaining skins.
2. Heat saucepan, then oil. Test oil by adding a small piece of *wonton* skin. If it sizzles and starts to turn golden, the oil is ready.
3. Reduce heat to medium. Add only 3 twists at a time and deep fry them 1 to 2 minutes; turn each twist over to cook evenly until they turn a pale gold. Do not burn them.
4. Drain on paper towels. While the twists are still hot, sift confectioners' sugar over both sides. Serve right away as a snack with or without tea. Or let them cool and store in a tightly closed canister or glass jar up to 6 weeks to keep them crispy. Resprinkle with sugar before serving.

VARIATION

Just before serving dribble honey over twists instead of sprinkling with confectioners' sugar.

TIPS

This recipe can easily be doubled or tripled.

To make simpler twists, put two halves together and twist them in the center in opposite directions to form a miniature bow tie. Moisten the center with water and press the halves together so they won't separate during deep frying.

Deep-Fried Sugared Walnuts *Syrup-coated walnuts are mouth-watering sweetmeats. Try them while sipping Chinese wine.*

½ pound shelled
    walnuts
⅓ cup sugar
¼ cup water
2   cups oil

PREPARATION: 5 minutes
    COOKING: 20 minutes
   CHILLING: 10 minutes
   UTENSILS: 1-quart saucepan with lid
    slotted spoon
    wax paper
    3-quart saucepan
    10-inch plate

STEPS

1. Cover the walnuts with cold water and bring to a boil in a 1-quart saucepan. Pour off the hot water and add sugar and ¼ cup cold water. Gently shake the pan to distribute the sugar; bring to boil again. Stir until all the sugar is absorbed.
2. Reduce heat to medium and simmer for 10 minutes. Scoop nuts out and spread them on wax paper. Pour any remaining syrup over them. Cool nuts near an open window for 10 minutes until the coating hardens.
3. Heat 3-quart saucepan, then oil for 5 minutes, over *moderate* heat. Test oil by adding a walnut. If it sizzles and turns brown, the oil is ready. Deep fry nuts 2 to 3 minutes only. Do not overcook; they burn easily! Remove the nuts immediately and cool them once again on wax paper. Store in a tightly closed glass jar or canister.

VARIATION

Instead of walnuts you can use pecans or blanched almonds.

PREPARE AHEAD: Sugared walnuts keep fresh for months.

Deep-Fried Sweet Wontons

Sweetened bean paste, red or black, is a popular filling for Chinese buns, pastries, and cakes. It is meltingly smooth inside a crispy fried wonton.

¼ cup sweetened red
    bean paste
12 *wonton* skins
3   cups oil

PREPARATION: 15 minutes
   COOKING: 2 to 6 minutes
   UTENSILS: 3-quart saucepan
            plate
            slotted spoon
            paper towels
     YIELD: 12 sweet *wontons*

STEPS

1. Roll 1 teaspoon of red bean paste into a round ball and repeat until there are 12. Set them aside.
2. With the *nonfloury side up* put a *wonton* skin in the palm of your hand. Put a red bean paste ball in its center. Wet a fingertip with water and gently pat around the ball. (This bit of moisture will help keep the skin closed during deep frying.) Follow **Steps 2** and **3** of *Wontons* (p. 38).
3. Heat saucepan, then oil. Test oil by adding a small piece of *wonton* skin. If it sizzles and starts to turn golden, the oil is ready. Reduce heat to medium. Add only 6 filled *wontons* at a time. Deep fry 1 to 3 minutes; turn each one over to fry evenly until they turn a light, golden brown. Do not overcook or the edges will burn. Remove at once. Drain on paper towels and serve hot.

TIP

Leftover sweet *wontons* can be refrigerated, well wrapped, for 2 to 3 days. Reheat them by deep frying for about 1 minute.

Chinese Sausage *Baked reddish brown Chinese sausages are crisp, chewy, and slightly dry. Steamed sausages are juicy and glisten with translucent dots of fat inside the casings. Each blends well with raw leeks and Chinese wine or plain rice.*

¼ **pound Chinese pork or duck liver sausages**
¼ **pound leeks**

PREPARATION: 5 minutes
BAKING: 12 minutes
STEAMING: 10 minutes
UTENSILS: aluminum foil
steamer
spatula
heatproof plate

STEPS

1. *To bake:* preheat oven to 400°F. Place sausages on aluminum foil. Bake 8 minutes on one side; turn them over and bake 4 to 5 minutes more. Slice sausages at a 45° slant into ⅛-inch pieces. Serve hot.

2. *To steam:* prepare a steamer (see p. 48). Place sausages on plate in steamer. Bring water to a boil. Reduce heat to medium and steam, covered, for 10 minutes. Slant-slice sausages into ¼-inch pieces. Serve hot.

3. Trim root end of leeks and discard. Cut off coarse green leaves to within 2 inches of the pale green section. Wash leeks under cold running water to remove any dirt. Slant-slice into ¼-inch pieces. Serve sausages hot; arrange a plate with the sausages on one side and the sliced leeks on the other side.

TIPS

Save the sausage drippings and recycle as oil for quick frying.

Use leftover sausage in Chinese Sausage Fried Rice (p. 27).

Steamed Beef Buns

10 plain oven-ready
 buns
1 tablespoon flour

MEAT FILLING
1 pound ground beef
 or ½ pound ground
 beef plus ½ pound
 ground pork
1 small onion, finely
 minced
1 clove garlic, minced
1 tablespoon water
1 teaspoon sherry
1 teaspoon salt

PREPARATION: 15 minutes
COOKING: 10 minutes
UTENSILS: steamer
 fork
 mixing bowl
 heatproof plate
 10 pieces of wax paper, each 2 inches square
YIELD: 10 buns

STEPS

1. Prepare a steamer (see p. 48).
2. With a fork or your fingers thoroughly combine the ingredients for the meat filling in a mixing bowl. Divide mixture into 10 parts. Firmly press, then roll each part (about 1 tablespoon) into a ball between your palms (moisten your hands from time to time with water). Repeat with the other parts of meat.
3. Follow **Step 3** of the recipe for Baked Bean Paste Buns (p. 136). Place each finished bun on a wax paper square. Place on a heatproof plate leaving space between buns. Put in steamer. Bring water to a boil. Reduce heat to medium and steam, covered, for 8 to 10 minutes.
4. Serve hot.

Baked Pork Buns *This snack is a savory variation of Baked Bean Paste Buns.*

10 plain oven-ready
   biscuits
1 tablespoon all-
   purpose flour

MEAT FILLING
½ pound ground pork
½ teaspoon salt
1 scallion, finely
   minced

OPTIONAL
2 teaspoons white
   sesame seeds

PREPARATION: 20 minutes
COOKING: 10 minutes
UTENSILS: mixing bowl
fork
rolling pin or tall glass
baking sheet
YIELD: 10 buns

STEPS

1. Preheat oven to 450° or the temperature listed on the tube of biscuits.
2. In a mixing bowl thoroughly combine all the ingredients for the meat filling with a fork or your fingers. Divide mixture into 10 parts. Firmly press, then roll each part (about 1 tablespoon) into a ball between your palms. Repeat with the other parts of meat.
3. Follow **Steps 3** and **4** of the recipe for Baked Bean Paste Buns (p. 136). The **Tips** apply as well.

Deep-Fried *Wontons*

12 *wontons* (p. 38)
3 cups oil

PREPARATION: see *Wontons* (p. 38)
COOKING: 6 to 8 minutes
UTENSILS: 3-quart saucepan
slotted spoon
paper towels
YIELD: 12 deep-fried *wontons*

STEPS

1. Heat saucepan, then oil. Reduce heat to medium. Add only 6 *wontons* at a time. Deep fry 3 to 4 minutes until they turn a light, golden brown. Drain on paper towels and serve hot.

TIP

Wontons keep warm up to 1 hour in a 250° oven.

Tea Leaf Eggs

In China, used tea leaves have many applications in the kitchen. Here is one of them. Tea leaf eggs require a long time but little effort to make. You will be delighted with the lovely brown crackle pattern that appears once you peel them.

6 hard-boiled eggs with shells

TEA LEAF MIXTURE
4 cups water
1 tablespoon soy sauce
1 tablespoon salt
2 star anise
¼ cup used black tea leaves or 3 black tea bags

PREPARATION: 5 minutes
  COOKING: 1 hour
  STEEPING: 6 to 8 hours or overnight
  UTENSILS: 2-quart saucepan with lid
      slotted spoon

STEPS

1. Gently crack the eggs all over. *Do not peel them.*
2. Combine the tea leaf mixture in a saucepan and bring to a boil. Add the eggs, turn heat to low, and simmer, covered, for 1 hour. Occasionally check water level and replace any that has boiled away.
3. Turn heat off. Let eggs steep, covered, 6 to 8 hours or preferably, overnight. Peel and eat plain, with your fingers. Serve hot or at room temperature.

PREPARE AHEAD: Keep eggs up to 1 week in the tea leaf mixture, refrigerated.

Deep-Fried Salted Peanuts

Crunchy, homemade salted nuts are fresher than the store-bought variety. Nibble them between meals or as a complement to Rice Porridge (p. 29), tea, or wine.

½ pound raw peanuts
2 cups oil
1 to 1½ teaspoons salt

COOKING: 5 minutes
UTENSILS: 3-quart saucepan
      slotted spoon
      paper towels

1. Heat saucepan, then oil, for 5 minutes. The oil is ready when a peanut sizzles and turns golden brown.
2. Reduce heat to medium. Add nuts and stir them constantly for 5 minutes until they turn a pale golden brown. Scoop them out, drain on paper towels, sprinkle with salt, and cool. Eat right away or store in a glass jar or canister for several weeks.

Shrimp Chips

Instead of potato chips try Oriental shrimp chips—crisp, pastel-colored puffs of ground shrimp and tapioca starch with a delicate and delicious taste. While you can buy them ready-to-eat in Chinese bakeries, you can buy them uncooked in cellophane-wrapped boxes in Chinese groceries and prepare them yourself. Serve these tidbits before a meal, as snacks, or at a tea or wine party. Fill a bamboo basket to pass around to your guests.

4 ounces shrimp chips, ready for frying
2 to 3 cups oil

UTENSILS: 3-quart saucepan or deep fryer
wire skimmer or slotted spoon
paper towels

STEPS

1. Heat saucepan, then oil, over medium heat for 5 minutes. To test oil, add one shrimp chip. When the chip sizzles, puffs up, and rises to the top, the oil is ready. The oil must not be too hot, for the shrimp chips will burn easily.
2. Add 5 or 6 chips at a time. In a matter of seconds the flat, waxy, oval little chips unfold and expand to 3 or 4 times their size and become bright and opaque. Quickly scoop them out and drain on paper towels. Serve as a snack right away or store up to a week in an airtight container to keep them crisp.

Store-to-Table:

THE CHINESE GROCERY
THE CHINESE DELICATESSEN
THE CHINESE BAKERY

Shopping in a Chinatown or Chinese market gives you the advantage of being able to buy not only Oriental vegetables, fresh-killed chickens, unfrozen ducks, and live fish, but also store-to-table items that need little or no preparation: crystallized ginger, canned lichees, frozen buns, soy sauce eggs, barbecued pork, "wife" cakes, and "honey bow ties." These ingredients are available in the Chinese grocery, delicatessen, and bakery. Such shops, whether separate entities or together under one roof, are a valuable time-saving source of ready-to-serve meal supplements that the Chinese frequently use.

THE CHINESE GROCERY

A Chinese grocery may be a small, traditional shop or a large, modern supermarket. We have divided the grocery into three sections: Canned and Bottled Products, Packaged Goods, Refrigerated and Freezer Sections. Because there are thousands of imports from the Far East, how will you know what to choose? To help you, we list here our recommendations for those products we feel you will like. They can be taken home and eaten as is, or be warmed, steamed, defrosted, or chilled, according to what you've bought. Some of these items are produced locally by specialty shops and factories: noodles, buns, dumplings; soybean milk, bean curd; sausages; cakes,

The Chinese Grocery

cookies, pastries; cooked meats, poultry, and animal parts. They are all extremely fresh, with no additives or preservatives, and can be considered virtually homemade!

Canned and Bottled Products

Imported canned products are a safe and speedy way to add to your family's meals. Most cans have attractive illustrations or photographs of the contents. The labels and ingredients are in English and sometimes in French, German, and Arabic as well. Serving instructions may also be given in English.

Many canned vegetarian products are available—either a mix of seasoned Oriental vegetables or a wheat gluten protein substitute for meat and poultry. To heat, simply remove the label by running the tip of a sharp knife along the seam. Put the opened can in a pan of boiling water for 10 minutes. Serve with rice and other dishes.

VEGETARIAN FOODS

Braised bamboo shoots or tips
Braised gluten
Hot *Papao Lajan* (braised vegetables and beans)
Vegetarian mock abalone
Sze Hsien Kow Fu (mixed vegetables with quail eggs)
Lo-Han-Chai (mixed vegetables)
Sueh-Tsai-Mow-Tow (green soy beans and snow cabbages)

The mixtures may contain bamboo shoots, lotus roots, baby sweet corn, straw mushrooms, deep-fried wheat gluten, fried bean curd, carrots, peanuts, and seasonings.

PICKLES AND PRESERVES

Among the varieties of sweet or sour pickles beloved in Chinese households, there are many excellent ones available in cans or bottles:

Preserved cucumbers (salty)
Preserved tea melons (also called sweetened cucumber)

Preserved ginger (often sold in decorative porcelain or
  pottery jars)
Preserved snow cabbages in brine
Pickled Chinese turnips
Mixed "gingers" in extra heavy syrup (ginger, cauliflower, cucumber, mustard greens, papaya, caram-
  bola, red pepper, carrots, lettuce stalks, lotus roots,
  and seasonings)

Serve these for a Chinese breakfast with rice porridge or
as side dishes for Eastern and Western meals.

FRUITS   Sweet desserts are not an after dinner habit in China.
Rather, fresh fruits in season are commonly offered: juicy
watermelons, peaches, apricots, crunchy mandarin "sand"
pears, pomegranates and red "dates," grapes, plums, persimmons, figs, apples, chestnuts, sweet turnips, petite mandarin
oranges, sweet cherries, mulberries and strawberries, pineapples, tangerines, mangoes, pomelos, star-fruit, lichees, loquats,
and many more. Most are available here in Oriental or His-
panic markets; many of the exotic types are imported, canned.
We feel sure you'll be delightfully surprised at the good taste
and fine quality of some of these canned varieties:

Arbutus in syrup (Chinese "strawberries" with an
  oval pit)
Longans in syrup
Loquats, whole, seedless, in heavy syrup
Lychee in heavy syrup (also spelled Lichee)
Mandarin orange segments in light syrup
Mandarin pears in light syrup
Flat peaches in syrup (white flesh)
Preserved kumquats in heavy syrup

These light, refreshing canned fruits from the Orient are
not as sweet as domestic products. Chill and serve them with
their syrup in a cut glass or porcelain bowl after an *Orient
Express* or Western meal.

Packaged Goods

The Chinese love to nibble on dried and preserved fruits, candies, melon seeds, and nuts rather than chocolates, chewing gum, or potato chips. We have found the quality of the following items to be excellent:

Dried fruits: apples, pears, apricots
Preserved fruits: persimmons, cherry-apples, sweet cured olives
Crystallized ginger
Candies made of coconut, peanuts, sesame seeds, walnuts, and dates
Peking haw slices and haw flakes
Sesame cookies
Fun Won rolls (cylindrical, flaky cookies in pretty tins)
Nuts: cashews, peanuts, walnuts, almonds
Salted dry melon seeds

All of these make lovely gifts and are kids' favorites.

Refrigerated and Freezer Sections

Next to the plain dough products, such as noodles and *wonton* skins, you will find a wide variety of ready-cooked cold and frozen items that can be reheated by boiling, steaming, and baking. Try to buy the foods prepared locally to insure freshness. Here are some suggestions:

STEAM OR BOIL	DEEP FRY	BAKE
Beef Meatball	Fantail Shrimp	Roast Pork Bun
Vegetable Bun	Shrimp Toast	Curry Beef
Peking Steam Roll	Eggroll	Turnover
Lotus Seed Bun	Shrimp *Wonton*	Beef Bun
Black or Red Bean Bun	Meat Dumpling	Scallion Pancake
Meat Dumpling	Chicken Roll	
Mandarin Pancakes	Taro Cake	ROOM TEMPERATURE
Shrimp Balls		Egg Custard
Fish Balls		Coconut Custard

When you go *Orient Express* marketing, try our carefully selected **Shopping Sources** listed in the **Appendix**. Take along our **Shopping List** and prepare one of your own. Bring cash; personal checks and credit cards may not be accepted in your area. Do carry an extra shopping bag. Have fun! And don't forget to pick up some of those wonderful Chinese beverages, wines and spirits (see pp. 172-184), and the teas we recommend.

Have you ever passed by the windows of a Chinese grocery or butcher shop and seen whole cooked chickens, ducks, and perhaps a roast pig hanging from metal hooks? Or have you looked at barbecued pork on skewers and innards on trays and wondered what they were and how they would taste? Well, you are at the Chinese "cooked meat" shop or delicatessen. Here, Chinese families buy ready-to-serve meat and poultry to supplement their home cooking.

If you step inside you may see a list of the items in the window written in English, with Chinese characters alongside. Next to each item will be the price, by the piece or pound. A sample list, which will vary from shop to shop, might read as follows:

WHITE CHOP CHICKEN
SALTED CHICKEN
CHICKEN WINGS & FEET
GIZZARDS/LIVER
SOY SAUCE EGGS
PIGEON/SQUAB
ROAST DUCK
SPECIAL DUCK
ROAST PIG
BARBECUED PORK
BARBECUED SPARERIBS

The Chinese Delicatessen

You may quickly get the impression that every part of pig, chicken and duck is sold. You are right!

If you look beyond the array of specially prepared foods made with closely guarded recipes, you will usually see a man deftly chopping and slicing with a large cleaver on a fat, round, tree-trunk section. You will be most impressed with his skill.

The poultry is sold whole—head and all—or in halves or quarters. The ducks and chickens will be chopped into bite-size pieces to be eaten with chopsticks. If you don't want your meat or poultry cut up, say so beforehand—the cleaver chops quickly! After you decide what you want, the man with the cleaver will put your "cooked meat" into a container or white carton and flap the lids shut. You might want to ask him for sauce, greens, or rice, which are often customary accompaniments to these delicatessen foods.

How do you tell the birds apart? The ducks have long beaks and necks, while the chickens have short, curved beaks and are round and plump. White chop chicken (actually boiled White-Cooked Chicken [p. 158]) is very pale with a pearly, yellow white skin. Its breast meat is juicy and succulent with a sweet, unpronounced taste. The salted chicken, usually a pale yellow, glistens with a film of oil; it naturally will taste salty. Chicken wings, gizzards/liver, and soy sauce eggs (*lu dan*) may all be dark brown from soy sauce stewing. You might find them next to trays of pig parts (tongue, feet, snout, and stomach) as well as chicken and duck feet. These items are inexpensive and very tasty.

The pigeon and squab (a young pigeon which weighs about a pound) are particularly favored by the Cantonese for family banquets and birthdays. They look like skinny Cornish hens and will have their heads and feet attached.

Buying a whole roast or special duck from a Chinese delicatessen is a real treat—a wonderful idea for a party or buffet (see **Menus**). Although not inexpensive, they don't cost much more than an uncooked bird and certainly much less than what you might pay in a Chinese restaurant. Your suburban Chinese grocer might order one for you, at no extra charge, from a supplier in the city, so inquire about this service.

Roast duck has a lacquery, red brown skin that is seasoned with soy sauce and some spices. Special duck is the flattened, pressed bird, with a circular-shaped body and a long, skinny neck. Because it resembles a Chinese lutelike musical instrument, the *piba*, it is called *piba* duck. While no notes will come from it, you will taste a more highly seasoned fowl that may be saltier and more pungent than the roast duck.

A whole, glazed roast pig hangs on a sturdy hook. With each purchase some of its crisp, crackled, golden yellow and brown skin with its fatty white layer will be cut off. In Chinese it is called "baked" or "golden" pig and should be reheated at home. How is it prepared? In large ovens with secret recipes. The shopkeeper would probably tell you: "I know how to cut it, not how to cook it!"

Barbecued pork (*cha siew*) hangs in strips that are red brown. (If bright red, they have probably been artificially colored.) Look for lean pieces with little or no fat. Point to the one you want or prepare your own the *Orient Express* way (p. 163). Barbecued spareribs may be hanging nearby. These can be chopped into finger-food sizes for you to serve at cocktail parties, wine parties (see **Menus**), buffets, children's birthdays, or picnics.

How do you serve these foods? Because they are fully cooked you do nothing more to them. Ideally, they should be served right away. However, if you're planning a party in the evening or the following day, refrigerate them, serve the chickens at room temperature and the innards and eggs at room temperature or cold. You can reheat the ducks briefly in a 250° oven and warm the pork products at a 350° temperature for 10 minutes. Serve these foods with plain rice, Steamed Buns (p. 42), Boiled *Bok Choy* (p. 67) or Boiled Spinach (p. 66), and a light soup. Try them for lunch, for part of a family-style supper, or for a more elaborate banquet (see **Menus**).

If it is difficult to get to a Chinese delicatessen, these foods can be made at home. While they won't be exact duplicates of what you'll find in the delicatessen, they'll be close enough. Check the home-style recipes that follow.

The next time you pass by the windows of a "cooked meat" shop, stop, go in, and buy something to take home and enjoy. Perhaps it will inspire you to try making some on your own.

White-Cooked Chicken
This Chinese style chicken-in-a-pot is boiled, simmered, and steeped in water. It is juicy, tender, and pale white with droplets of fat shining on the velvety smooth skin. The meat is also white with a touch of pink. Two spicy dips accent this unadorned bird.

2 to 3-pound chicken with giblets (preferably fresh killed)
3 tablespoons salt
¼ cup sherry
water to cover

GARLIC DIP
¼ cup soy sauce
4 cloves garlic, minced

GINGER DIP
¼ cup soy sauce
2 teaspoons ginger, minced

PREPARATION: 10 minutes
SALTING: 20 minutes to overnight
COOKING: 25 minutes
STEEPING: 20 minutes to 2 hours
UTENSILS: 5 to 7-quart heavy casserole with lid

STEPS

1. Wash and pat chicken dry. Remove fat from the cavity. Rub the salt on the bird's skin, inside the cavity, and on the giblets. Set aside for 20 minutes or refrigerate overnight.
2. Put the chicken in the casserole, add the wine, and cover with cold water. Bring to a boil. Reduce heat to medium and simmer for 20 minutes. Turn heat off and let steep, covered, for 20 minutes to 2 hours.
3. Combine ingredients for each dip.
4. When chicken is cool, drain and reserve broth. Cut chicken into chunks and serve at room temperature with dips in small, shallow bowls.

TIPS

Strain the broth and use it as a stock for soups.

The cold chicken meat can be added to Celery Salad (p. 78) or Cold Noodles with Sesame Paste (p. 34).

Soy Sauce Chicken Wings

1 pound chicken wings
Soy Sauce Stock to
cover (p. 4)

PREPARATION: 5 minutes
COOKING: 15 minutes
STEEPING: 15 minutes
UTENSILS: saucepan with lid
slotted spoon

STEPS

1. Bring the stock to a boil. Wash wings. Cut them at the joints, add to the stock, and bring to boil again.
2. Reduce heat to medium and simmer, covered, for 15 minutes. Turn heat off and let wings steep in covered stock for at least 15 minutes. Remove from the stock and serve hot or at room temperature.

TIPS

Leftover chicken wings can be kept in cooled stock in the refrigerator up to 1 week. To reheat, bring the stock to just below the boiling point. Drain wings and serve.

This recipe can be either doubled or tripled for parties or for buffets.

Soy Sauce Hard-Boiled Eggs *Delicious, firm-textured soy sauce eggs (lu dan) are sold in Chinatown markets and in street stalls just as they were in China. They are easy to make at home, too.*

4 or 6 hard-boiled
eggs, peeled
Soy Sauce Stock to
cover (p. 4)

COOKING: 10 minutes
STEEPING: 6 to 8 hours, or overnight
UTENSILS: saucepan with lid
slotted spoon

STEPS

1. Bring the stock to a boil. Add eggs and bring to boil again.
2. Reduce heat to medium and simmer, covered, for 10 minutes. Turn heat off and steep eggs in covered stock at room temperature for 6 to 8 hours or overnight. Remove eggs from the stock and slice in halves or quarters. Serve hot or at room temperature.

PREPARE AHEAD: 2 to 3 days in stock in the refrigerator.

Soy Sauce Chicken Gizzards *These inexpensive chicken innards take on a new dimension after stewing in a spiced Soy Sauce Stock. Serve as tasty morsels at a buffet or outing.*

1 pound chicken
gizzards
Soy Sauce Stock to
cover (p. 4)

OPTIONAL
2 cloves garlic,
smashed, or
1 teaspoon red
pepper flakes

SUBSTITUTE
Use ½ pound each of
gizzards and chicken
hearts.

PREPARATION: 3 minutes
COOKING: 15 minutes
UTENSILS: 3-quart saucepan with lid
slotted spoon

STEPS

1. Bring Soy Sauce Stock and garlic or pepper to a boil.
2. Wash gizzards and add to saucepan. Bring stock to boil again. Reduce heat to medium and simmer, covered, for 15 minutes.
3. Remove garlic or pepper from stock. Slice gizzards into ¼-inch pieces and serve hot, cold, or at room temperature.

TIP

Spear them with toothpicks to serve as hors d'oeuvres at a wine party, or eat them with a fork or chopsticks when served with rice as part of a meal.

Barbecued Pork Spareribs

Barbecued spareribs are usually eaten plain, with rice. They are not eaten with the "duck sauce" and hot mustard that are served to Westerners in Chinese restaurants. Home-cooked, red brown ribs are so luscious, you won't need any accompaniments!

2 pounds baby pork spareribs

MARINADE
¼ cup hoisin sauce
¼ cup scallions, finely sliced
3 tablespoons sherry
1 tablespoon soy sauce
1 teaspoon salt
1 teaspoon sugar
1 clove garlic, minced

PREPARATION: 15 minutes
MARINATING: 2 to 48 hours
COOKING: 30 minutes
UTENSILS: bread loaf pan or plastic bag
aluminum foil or baking rack
baking sheet
tongs

STEPS

1. Trim fat from spareribs and cut them apart, lengthwise.
2. Mix marinade ingredients well and coat ribs thoroughly. Marinate in a covered loaf pan or knotted plastic bag in the refrigerator for 1 hour; turn ribs over and leave for 1 hour more or up to 48 hours. Turn ribs occasionally.
3. Preheat oven to 400°. Put aluminum foil or preferably a baking rack (see **Tips**) on the baking sheet and spread the ribs on it. Bake on one side for 15 minutes; turn them over and bake for 15 minutes more. Serve hot or at room temperature.

TIPS

When you trim the spareribs save the odd pieces of meat and fat for use in pork stock.

Cut the ribs apart close to the bone on one side, rather

than between the bones. Cutting them this way makes it easier to eat the meat.

To prepare a baking rack from aluminum foil: Measure the foil to twice the length of your baking sheet. Fold it into pleats ½ inch high and 1½ inches apart. Turn up the edges of the foil to a height of 1 to 1½ inches. When you put it on the baking sheet, lay the ribs *across* the peaks of the foil. The valleys will catch the drippings and you won't have to clean your baking sheet afterward.

For added flavor smear any excess marinade over the ribs with the washed root end of a fat scallion—it's a natural brush!

For home buffets, chop the ribs into 2 to 3-inch pieces and serve at room temperature.

To reheat ribs, put them in a 350° oven for 10 minutes.

PREPARE AHEAD: 2 days marinating or baked.

Barbecued Pork

There's nothing as mouth watering as the aroma of home-cooked barbecued pork. This dish is so easy and rewarding you'll be wise to make double or triple the amount—it will disappear very quickly.

1 pound pork, in 4 ×
1½-inch strips

MARINADE
2 tablespoons catsup
2 tablespoons sherry
2 tablespoons soy
sauce
4 cloves garlic, minced
1 teaspoon salt

PREPARATION: 10 minutes
MARINATING: 2 to 48 hours
COOKING: 40 minutes
UTENSILS: bread loaf pan or plastic bag
aluminum foil or baking rack
baking sheet
long-handled fork

STEPS

1. Mix marinade ingredients well and coat pork strips thoroughly and evenly by turning them in the mixture. Marinate in a covered loaf pan or knotted plastic bag in the refrigerator for 2 to 48 hours; turn pork strips occasionally.

2. Preheat oven to 400°. Put aluminum foil or preferably a baking rack (see **Tips** for Barbecued Pork Spareribs [p. 161]) on the baking sheet and lay pork strips on it. Bake for a total of 40 minutes; baste and turn the strips *every 10 minutes*. Allow to cool before slicing into ¼-inch pieces. Serve hot.

TIPS

Use either pork butt, shoulder, rib end, or boneless loin.

To reheat barbecued pork, put strips in a 350° oven for 10 minutes. If frozen, thaw; then reheat.

Serve as a snack with Steamed Buns or as part of a buffet or party meal.

PREPARE AHEAD: 2 days marinating or baked.

Barbecued Chicken Drumsticks

2 pounds small chicken drumsticks

MARINADE
¼ cup hoisin sauce
¼ cup scallions, finely sliced
2 tablespoons sherry
1 tablespoon soy sauce
1 teaspoon salt
1 teaspoon sugar
2 cloves garlic, minced

PREPARATION: 5 minutes
MARINATING: 1 hour
COOKING: 30 minutes
UTENSILS: bread loaf pan or plastic bag
aluminum foil or baking rack
baking sheet
tongs

STEPS

1. Wash the drumsticks and pat them dry. Cut 2 diagonal slashes 1 inch long and ¼ inch deep on the fat part of each drumstick.

2. Mix marinade ingredients well and coat the drumsticks thoroughly. Marinate them in a covered loaf pan or knotted plastic bag at room temperature for 1 hour, turning them over once.

3. Preheat oven to 400°. Place aluminum foil or preferably a baking rack (see **Tips** for Barbecued Pork Spareribs, p. 161) on the baking sheet and lay drumsticks on it. Bake on one side for 15 minutes; turn them over and bake for 15 minutes more. Serve hot or at room temperature.

TIP

Tuck a few of these drumsticks into a picnic basket or lunch box.

Crispy Duck

*To transform a simple Steamed Duck into a succulent, banquet-style dish, briefly deep fry and serve it with soft Steamed Buns (p. 42), dainty Scallion Brushes (see **Tips**), and thick sweet hoisin sauce or a salt-and-pepper dip. Your guests will be very impressed.*

Steamed Duck
2 **to 3 cups oil**

DIPS
1 **tablespoon salt plus
½ teaspoon ground
black pepper**
or
½ **cup hoisin sauce**

PREPARATION: see Steamed Duck (p. 60)
    COOKING: 10 minutes
    UTENSILS: electric frying pan or heavy 10 to 12-inch skillet
          with lid
          long-handled spoon
          paper towels

STEPS

1. Heat oil for 5 minutes. Pat the duck dry and cover it immediately in the pan or skillet. Lift lid and deep fry *breast side down* for 2 to 3 minutes; then turn the duck over and deep fry 2 minutes more until the skin is golden brown, taut, and crispy. If the oil doesn't completely cover the duck, baste duck a couple of times during the second frying.

2. Serve hot with either dip. Pull the meat off the bones or cut it the same way as Steamed Duck. If you wish, serve it with 10 Steamed Buns and 10 Scallion Brushes. Arrange the buns, curved sides out, around the duck, alternated with the scallions. Place small bowls of hoisin sauce within reach. Tuck a small piece of meat and skin into an opened bun and smear it with a dollop of hoisin sauce picked up with a scallion brush which you push into the bun as well.

TIPS

Save the carcass for use in Duck Bone Soup (p. 123).

To make Scallion Brushes: Wash and trim 10 scallions. Use only the white ends and cut them into 1½-inch lengths. Make 1 inch deep criss-cross cuts into the end of the whitest part. Use them as decorative touches with other dishes or to smear hoisin sauce on Steamed Buns for Crispy Duck. They can be made ahead of time and kept in a bowl of cold water in the refrigerator until you are ready to use them. Pat dry first.

If you can only think of almond and fortune cookies when you think of Chinese pastries, you're in for a pleasant surprise. Fortune cookies, always offered after meals in Chinese-American restaurants, were "invented" in this country. Traditionally, the Chinese bakery or pastry store (*ping dian*) has specialized in and made most of its money from wife cakes, moon cakes, and New Year cakes.

Wife cakes (*lao p'o ping*) are sent by a bride's family to all her friends to announce an engagement or marriage. This gesture might take place a month or up to two years in advance, as well as on the wedding day itself. Hundreds of boxes of four cakes, 3 inches round, are delivered by the family. Pork and preserved winter melon are the usual ingredients of each wife cake.

In China two splendid mythological creatures symbolize the married couple: the benevolent dragon (*lung*), king of the animals, and the beautifully plumed, long-tailed phoenix (*fong*), queen of the birds. Because the bulk of the business in Chinese bakeries relates to marriage, you may find that either the dragon, the phoenix, or both form part of the store's name and are often pictured on the brightly decorated boxes of *lao p'o ping* sent around in honor of the happy occasion.

The Chinese Bakery

The Moon Festival falls on the fifteenth day of the Eighth month on the lunar calendar, sometime during September. Traditionally, Chinese families gathered at reunions and parties to celebrate the appearance of the roundest and brightest full harvest moon. One month prior to this autumn festival, Chinese bakeries are filled with rounded moon cakes (*yue ping*).

Moon cakes are rarely baked at home because they require many ingredients, special wooden or metal forms, and ovens. Instead, they are bought and presented as gifts, four to a box to symbolize the four blessings: long life, prosperity, joy, and happiness. A quartet of presents, including moon cakes, might also be exchanged: wine, tea, dried Chinese mushrooms, "1,000 Year" eggs, or ham. The moon cakes, about 3½ × 1½ inches, are cut into two or four pieces and may be served with warmed rice wine. Ideally, they should be eaten while viewing a luminescent moon in a clear sky.

There are two kinds of moon cakes. One has a yellow brown, hard-glazed crust and is round with scalloped edges; the other has a flakier, gray white crust in a round shape, closer in appearance to the moon. Fillings include sweetmeats, lard, nuts, minced ham, egg yolks, bean paste, sugar, and dried fruit. Chinese characters in raised dough on top describe the main ingredient: "Ham Moon Cake" or "Yellow Bean Paste Moon Cake." The Chinese characters might also advertise the name of the shop.

Another festive occasion, the Chinese New Year, is also marked by the appearance in bakeries of special cakes from late January to mid-February. These "cakes" (*nian gao*) are steamed, sweet, flat squares of glutinous rice powder and sugar. Saltier versions with vegetables, turnips, or taro are sold by the pound.

If you're not getting married or have missed the Moon Festival in autumn and the New Year in winter, what else might you find in a Chinese bakery? Plenty. In a well-stocked store you might be able to buy 50 or more *ping* (cakes, cookies, and pastries) of Eastern origin. You can have a serendipitous, lip-smacking adventure trying them; serve them at home as snacks, at tea and wine parties (see **Menus**), or give them as presents—a traditional Chinese custom.

Generally, Chinese bakeries do not resemble Western bakeries. You will not find Western breads, rolls, fruit pies, layer cakes filled with butter cream, meringues, sugary confections, birthday cakes with icing or whipped cream, tiny cookies, or chocolaty morsels. Instead, you will discover plain cookies, little custard pies, meat buns, and turnovers; deep-fried crullers; rice, nut, and melon pastries; round and oval buns with sweet or savory insides; simple sponge cakes; and steamed "jellies," to name just a few. These small pastries are sold individually, not by weight.

Sometimes the ingredients are rich, heavy, and lavish; sometimes they are plain and light: bits of pork, chicken, beef, or ham; salted egg yolks; rice and wheat flour; nuts (almonds, cashews, peanuts, walnuts); lotus seeds; preserved eggs; white or black sesame seeds; lard; red beans; ginger; sugar or honey; sweetened red, black, or yellow bean paste; and dried fruits.

Little signs in English and Chinese usually describe the *ping* and list the cost. Most items are reasonably priced from 25¢ to $1.25 each. For your enjoyment we recommend a baker's dozen of any of these Chinese pastries:

◆ Light, deep-fried twists of dough made sticky with a gilding of honey, called "Honey Bow Ties."

◆ Southern-style coconut shreds, or "Coconut Mountain": a crisp, white, macaroonlike confection with a cherry on its "peak."

◆ Crumbly baked cookies glazed with egg yolk; a walnut, peanut, almond, or cherry in the centers.

◆ Boxes of 50 almond cookies, thin and delicate—a thrifty idea for a large party or buffet.

- Sand-colored round cookies of pressed and molded almond and rice powder, with raised Chinese characters on top—it melts in your mouth and is called "almond paste."
- Savory pastries: Yellow Bean Paste, and Black Bean.
- Moon cakes: Egg Yolk Lotus, Mixed Nut Special, and Black Bean Moon.
- Fortune cookies: whole, or broken (in bags at half or one-third the price).
- Cinnamon twirls: yellow with red brown swirls (also called "cow ear" cookies in Chinese).
- Deep-fried, pastel shrimp chips (to make your own, see p. 145).
- Baked beef or curry turnovers.
- Roast pork buns.
- Pastel-hued squares or diamonds of gelatinous "jellies" in window trays—often made from steamed rice powder, brown or white sugar, and food coloring.

While visiting the Chinese bakery, you will be enchanted by small, hard, yellow-glazed molded figures of chubby fish and seated, smiling Buddhas with bean eyes and red blossoms stamped on them. These will make nice souvenirs of your visit. They are made to last for years, are practically tasteless, and are said to bring good luck.

Will you find anything in a Chinese bakery for a birthday party? A Chinese birthday "cake" is usually a bowl of long, unbroken noodles which symbolize longevity. However, why not add an Oriental touch to your festivities by also serving a variety of Chinese *ping*?

Beverages: Hot, Warm, and Cold

Chinese liquid refreshments include a wide range of products as ancient as tea and wine and as new as instant mixes. Whether you serve them hot, warm, or cold, they will add pleasure to your enjoyment of Chinese food.

TEA (*CHA*) Tea is the national beverage of the Chinese people; it is also the number one choice worldwide of liquid refreshment after water. In China, it was discovered that leaves from the tea plant (*Camellia sinensis*) added flavor, aroma, and hue to boiling water. They also had a stimulating effect on the drinker as well. In fact, tea was originally valued as a medicinal brew.

Green, Black, and Oolong Teas Chinese tea leaves, green, black, and *oolong* ("black dragon") come from the same Oriental plant but are processed differently. Black tea is fermented, green tea is not, and *oolong* is partially fermented. In China black and *oolong* are called "red" tea, because of their color after brewing.

The best green tea leaves are those tender ones picked by hand from the very top of each branch from tea bushes. After processing, they appear in shades from bright to dull gray green; they are often flat, smooth, and shiny. Once boiling water is poured over them, the green tea leaves unfurl fully. The brew is pale with a greenish tint. It has a light, cooling, sharp and clean taste. Green tea is the daily drink of the majority of Chinese.

Beverages: Hot, Warm, and Cold

Black and *oolong* tea leaves are coal dark or soot gray, curled, shriveled, and withered. Black tea is a deep coppery or amber red with a heavy, warming, full-bodied, slightly acid taste. Fermentation increases the tannic acid content. Black tea, the tea that is usually served in Chinese restaurants in America, is preferred by many Americans and the English. In China it is served infrequently—perhaps during the summer, hot or iced, or maybe during festive occasions such as weddings and New Year's banquets. *Oolong*, more golden in tint, has an intermediate flavor.

Flower Teas

The scented flower teas are another delightful family of teas. These are blends of green or black leaves that are mixed with or exposed to the fragrant Eastern blossoms of jasmine, rose, magnolia, and lichee.

Leaves, Bags, and Bricks

Chinese teas now come in either the traditional loose form, in compressed bricks, and even in tea bags. Loose tea leaves may be sold in canisters, paper packets, boxes, or by weight from large glass apothecary jars or cans. Many Chinese teas come in tea bags that are quick, neat, and convenient and that eliminate the use of a teapot or the need to measure loose tea for each cup. However, they are more expensive than loose or brick tea. Compressed or brick tea (*beeng cha*) is made from lesser grades of whole or broken older leaves and stems. These are steamed and compressed by machine into hard bricks that may be round, square, or spherical; they have to be cut with a knife or broken off with the fingers.

Strongly flavored *pu-erh* tea from Yunnan Province comes either loose, in tea bags, or in bricks. The brick form is shaped like a disk, about 9 inches across and 1½ inches thick. It is sold in Chinese markets in a gaily decorated box or plainly wrapped in tissue paper and cellophane.

Buying Tea

To get fresh tea, shop for it in a Chinese store where there is a quick turnover. Avoid dusty boxes and canisters that may have been sitting on the shelf for months. Fresh tea always tastes better than stale tea. If you have purchased tea in a tightly closed metal container, leave it there and stick a label with the date on the bottom as a reminder. If it came in plain paper or a box, transfer it to a canister or glass jar with a lid. Because volatile oils in tea evaporate and spoil its freshness after six months and because tea leaves absorb other odors, it is doubly important to store it properly, away from heat.

One pound of tea can make at least 200 cups, so buy only a small amount, 1 or 2 ounces. Share a large purchase with someone or give it away—a gift of tea is a gesture of friendship in the Orient. After a year, throw it out!

Selecting a Tea

How do you know which tea of the many hundreds available you should select? In the better stocked stores you may be overwhelmed by an array of shelf after shelf of bright tins and canisters, painted bamboo containers, decorated porcelain jars, and plain paper packets—all filled with tea! They are imported from the People's Republic of China, Hong Kong, and Taiwan. Not only are the displays colorful—they are confusing to the novice.

When selecting tea, we suggest you start with green tea, which is the most popular in China. Choose a canister or package simply labeled Green Tea, without any modifying adjectives. Or you might choose another palate-pleasing green tea, the aromatic Jasmine, with dried white petals in it. After experimenting with green tea, try a plain black tea (*oolong*) or lichee. Becoming a tea connoisseur can be as complicated as tasting wines, so start slowly. To get started, why not give a tea party for your friends? (See **Menus**.)

Choosing a Teapot

Properly brewed tea requires a glazed or unglazed pottery, porcelain, or glass teapot. Avoid metals (including silver) which will adversely affect the tea's taste and color. Antique or new, a Chinese teapot is always an authentic touch!

Before and after each brewing, wash the inside and outside of your teapot with hot water to remove any odor and flavor from a previous infusion. (Be sure to remove all the tea leaves.) Do not use soap or detergents. To remove stains or sour smells from your teapot, use a solution of 1 quart water and ¼ cup baking soda.

Brewing Tea Some people like strong tea; others prefer it weak. Some tea drinkers prefer second and third brewings to the first. The longer you allow it to steep in the pot, the stronger it becomes. Green tea is more potent than black. Use ½ teaspoon green leaves, or 1 teaspoon black or *oolong* leaves per 6 ounces of water. A small, slope-sided Chinese teacup holds 4 ounces of liquid, while a larger Chinese tea mug with handle and lid and Western teacups hold twice as much.

Water In China water for tea was traditionally considered every bit as important as the tea leaves. Water was often collected from special springs, streams, and famous wells noted for their lightness and clarity. It was sometimes obtained by melting freshly fallen snow. It was even gathered from the morning dew. Sometimes it was stored or buried for years in precious urns and porcelain vases.

At home use cold tap water. Let it first run for a few seconds. Bring the water to a brisk boil. Scald the teapot and, if you wish, the teacups to eliminate any odor from the previous tea and to preheat the utensils. (To scald, pour boiling water on the inside and outside of the teapot and cups.) Add leaves, tea bags, or chunks of brick tea and the freshly boiled water. Cover the teapot and steep 3 to 5 minutes until the leaves sink to the bottom.

Serving Tea In China tea is not sipped during the meal as it is in Chinese restaurants in America. Rather, it is served before breakfast, after meals, away from the dining table, and between meals. Whenever a guest arrives, it is customary to offer a cup of tea. It is not unusual to find a pot of tea visible in Chinese homes, shops, offices, and factories.

Green tea is served without sugar, lemon, milk, or cream. Black tea may be taken with sugar and lemon. When tea is poured it is done slowly and gracefully with one hand lightly touching the top of the teapot cover.

More "Teas"

Many other ingredients besides tea leaves are infused with boiling water to make a kind of tea, including certain nuts, seeds and flowers. One of these, dried chrysanthemum blossoms, is sold in Chinese apothecary shops. This brew is a delicious, fragrant, light tea which aids digestion. Its white petals and golden yellow centers puff and swell in hot water—they look lovely as they float to the top of the teapot. Buy this costly ingredient an ounce at a time.

Chrysanthemum tea is usually served with rough, pale gold or light brown chunks of unrefined "rock sugar," or *bing tang* in Chinese, meaning "ice sugar." The lumps do look like pieces of frozen water. Crush a lump into bits and add to the teapot after the dried flowers and before pouring the boiling water. Steep 5 minutes and serve. Store chrysanthemum tea like other teas.

Instant chrysanthemum crystals that contain both flowers and sugar are also available. Mix 2 tablespoons of the crystals with either 1 cup of boiling or iced water to make a pleasant, sweet drink.

SOYBEAN MILK

Ivory-colored soybean milk is sold in Chinatown stores in the refrigerated case alongside packaged bean curd, noodles, or regular milk and juices or soda. It comes in pint and quart containers.

Sweetened soybean milk can be drunk hot or cold. To warm it up, put it in a heatproof container, uncovered, over low heat. Do not boil. In North China soybean milk is commonly served hot at breakfast; a long, deep-fried cruller is usually dipped into it just as we dunk donuts into coffee.

Now that we have established that neither tea, water, milk, coffee, or soda is consumed during a Chinese meal—what do they drink? Soup is the main liquid. It appears with the other courses and serves as a beverage throughout the meal. However, during a family-style meal and most certainly at a birthday or wedding banquet, wine will be served so that guests can toast one another's health and future happiness.

WINES AND SPIRITS (*CHIEW*)

A single word, *chiew,* in the Cantonese dialect, and *jiu,* in Mandarin, means any wine, spirit, liquor, or alcoholic beverage. These may be gentler wines of only 14% alcohol by volume or stronger spirits of 100 proof (50% alcohol) or higher. Wine is essential to the Chinese cook for marinating meats and fowl, deodorizing fish, and pickling vegetables. But it also appears as a drink at special occasions.

Chinese wines and spirits are more likely to be fermented from rice rather than grapes and distilled from millet and sorghum. There are four main categories of *chiew:* yellow, white, medicinal, and fruit. One of the most popular table wines is the celebrated Shao Hsing yellow wine, which is actually a rich amber in color. It is made in the city of Shao Hsing (near the eastern seacoast, south of Hangchow) from glutinous rice and waters of Jian Lake which are said to insure its fine quality. It does double duty as both a wine for cooking and imbibing. There are two types: regular and *hua tiao,* meaning "carved flower," which is the finer and older of the two. All Shao Hsing must be aged for at least 10 years. Imitations are imported from Taiwan. Whenever one of our recipes calls for pale dry sherry, it is a substitute for yellow rice wine. If you can find the real thing, by all means use it!

Two of the white *chiew* available here are the well-known potent spirits *kaoliang,* distilled from sorghum, and Mou Tai, distilled from combinations of wheat and millet or surghum. Both are colorless and look like water, gin, or vodka. *Kaoliang* often forms a base for medicinal wines. Mou Tai is made in the small town of that name in the northern part of Kweichow Province, from grains and a famed spring water. The 106-proof spirit has a powerful aroma and kick; sip it with caution.

Each region has its own specialty and this is particularly true of the fruit wines. In the countryside peasants and farmers frequently make wine at home from rice, oranges, plums, persimmons, lichees, pineapples, coconuts, and even flowers, to mention just a few. A Peking dry white grape wine is now sold in the United States, as is the much-favored Mei Kuei Lu, "rose dew" wine. This potation has a clear *kaoliang* base to which fresh rose petals and sugar are added.

Medicinal wines are often strong and bitter. Wu Chia Pi, red in color (106 proof) and Chu Yeh Ching, green gold (92.9 proof) are two of the more palatable types sold here.

The city of Tsingtao in Shantung Province is the source of European-style beer and Chinese vodkas, the legacy respectively of Germans and Russians who went there in the early years of this century. Today, beer is being brewed in the Bavarian-style brewery in Tsingtao and is available nationally in selected stores, bars, and restaurants. The pure artesian waters of the area are blended with distilled wheat to make an 80-proof vodka that is said to compare favorably with the Russian original.

Serving Chinese Wines

Because they are drunk straight, Chinese wines are always served with food. But they will not appear at a Western-style cocktail party; the Chinese rarely drink their wines standing, but rather when seated around the dinner table.

Mixers, tonic, soda, water, other alcohols, ice, fruits, juices, or condiments are not combined with Chinese wines and spirits. Therefore, wines should not be consumed on an empty stomach. It is the custom to take a bite of food first, then a sip of wine. Some wines are warmed and are therefore even more potent; the alcohol enters the bloodstream more rapidly. Wine and food go together in China (see our suggestions for a wine party under **Menus**). When wine is served at a banquet the toast is *kan pei* or "bottoms up," and is often involved in a finger-guessing game where the loser has to drink up.

Shao Hsing should be drunk warm. Put it in a heatproof measuring cup or tall container. Place this in a 2-quart saucepan and fill it with water so the container is steady and doesn't wobble or float. Bring it to a temperature of 98° to 100° over low heat. Don't boil it or the alcohol will evaporate. After you serve your guests (liqueur glasses would be fine), replace the wine container in the hot water to keep it warm. Traditionally, wine was served from slender-spouted porcelain, pewter, or silver wine pots and poured into tiny cups. A Chinese wine will make an *Orient Express* meal even more authentic.

JUICES China's cornucopia of fruit has been squeezed, packaged, and exported. Slender bottles of lichee, sand pear, arbutus, and other exotic fruit juices are sold in Chinese groceries. Unusual canned drinks, served hot or chilled according to directions on their labels, are prune, black sesame seed, red bean and pressed sugar-cane juice. Some will taste very new, and are worth a try.

Almond "tea," sugar cane and imperatae, and chrysanthemum are instant mixes sold in powder, granular, and crystal form. Look for them next to teas. Add boiled or iced water, stir, and serve. They will expand your repertory of summertime thirst-quenchers and wintertime warmers. Juice, soybean milk, *cha* or *chiew*—the choice is up to you!

We want to thank Albert Jacques Amsellem of China Wine & Liquor Co., New York, for his generously offered information on Chinese wines and spirits.

Instant Almond "Tea"

During the chill, dry winter in North China, fragrant cups of steaming hot almond "tea" were sold to early morning shoppers in the marketplace or to worshippers at temples. Almond "tea," made from ground nuts, was a pick-me-up like coffee. It was more common than tea brewed from tea leaves, because almonds are native to the North, while tea bushes grow in the warm, wet lands of the South.

However, northern almonds are different from the kind we know. They are heart-shaped, ½ inch across, with a bittersweet taste. Some are now being imported from the People's Republic of China.

Try this white almond powder to get a similar effect.

¼ cup almond powder
5 tablespoons sugar
¼ cup cold water
4 cups water

PREPARATION: 5 minutes
UTENSILS: saucepan
4-cup measuring cup
YIELD: 4 cups

STEPS

1. Bring water to a boil.
2. Pour the almond powder into the measuring cup. Add sugar and cold water and stir until the powder and sugar are *completely dissolved.*
3. Simultaneously add the boiling water and stir the almond powder mixture. Pour into cups and serve hot.

TIPS

A salty snack would commonly be nibbled along with this sweet drink because the Chinese appreciate contrasts. To them the idea of having coffee with sugar and a sweet pastry is odd. Try munching Salted Peanuts (p. 144) or crackers with this almond "tea" and pour it from a teapot as they do in China!

Almond powder is available in jars, tins, or packages, usually in the tea section of Chinese markets.

Sugar Cane and Imperatae

Beverage *The juices of two tropical grasses, sugar cane and imperata, were long appreciated in China for their cooling, thirst-quenching properties. They were a summertime favorite, sold from streetcorner stands in the southern provinces.*

At times the stout, jointed stalks of sugar cane were pressed in front of the customer. Today light brown granules of 95% sugar cane mixed with 5% imperata are the instant version of this old-time drink. Your friends will find this pale gold liquid quite refreshing and, surprisingly, not too sweet.

4 packets (0.7 ounces each) or ½ cup sugar cane and imperatae beverage
1 cup water
3 cups ice water
ice cubes

PREPARATION: 5 minutes
UTENSILS: saucepan
           4-cup measuring cup
YIELD: 4 cups

STEPS

1. Bring water to a boil.
2. Pour the granules into the measuring cup. Add boiling water and stir until the granules are *completely dissolved*. Add ice water, stir, and pour into tall glasses with 2 to 4 ice cubes per glass. Serve cold.

TIP

This beverage mix is sold in packets or loose, in boxes or tins, in the tea section of Chinese markets.

GROCERIES The Chinese groceries, delicatessens, bakeries, wine and liquor stores, and specialty shops listed in our book have been visited personally and selected with care. The standards included completeness of inventory, ease of shopping, well-organized displays, cleanliness, and pleasant surroundings and staff. All things change, but as of this writing we hope you will agree with our recommendations. Have fun!

CALIFORNIA

KWAN LEE LUNG CO.
801 North Hill Street
Los Angeles, CA 90012

WING CHONG LUNG CO.
922 S. San Pedro Street
Los Angeles, CA 90015

YEE SING CHONG CO., INC.
966 North Hill Street
Los Angeles, CA 90012

YICK CHONG COMPANY
423 J Street
Sacramento, CA 95814
(Chinese delicatessen
available)

CHONG IMPORTS
Chong Kee Jan Co., Inc.
838 Grant Avenue
San Francisco, CA 94108
(two levels; wide selection
of Chinese bowls,
tea sets, etc.)

DUPONT MARKET
1100 Grant Avenue
San Francisco, CA 94133
(Chinese delicatessen
available)

GOURMET KING
1131 Grant Avenue
San Francisco, CA 94133
(Chinese delicatessen
available)

Shopping Sources

ITALIAN MARKET, INC.
966 Grant Avenue
San Francisco, CA 94108
(Chinese delicatessen
available)

KENSON TRADING CO.
1251 Stockton Street
San Francisco, CA 94133
and
434 Clement Street
San Francisco, CA 94118

LUN WAH CO.
1117 Stockton Street
San Francisco, CA 94133
(Chinese delicatessen
available)

MAN FUNG CHINA TRADING
CO., INC.
1301 Stockton Street
San Francisco, CA 94133

MANLEY PRODUCE CO.
1101 Grant Avenue
San Francisco, CA 94108

KWONG ON TEONG CO.
718 Webster Street
Oakland, CA 94607

NEW SANG CHONG MARKET
377 Eighth Street
Oakland, CA 94607
(Chinese delicatessen
available)

ORIENT GROCERY
337 Eighth Street
Oakland, CA 94607

ILLINOIS

MAN SUN WING COMPANY
2229 S. Wentworth
Chicago, IL 60616

MARYLAND

FAR EAST HOUSE
Maryland & North Avenue
Baltimore, MD 21201

MASSACHUSETTS

WING WING IMPORTED
GROCERIES
79 Harrison Avenue
Boston, MA 02111

WOK TALK
1351 Washington Street
Route 16
W. Newton Square, MA 02165

NEW JERSEY

LAVONE INTERNATIONAL
INC.
3 Railroad Plaza
New Brunswick, NJ 08901

ORIENTAL FOOD
985 Main Avenue
Passaic, NJ 07055

NEW YORK

C.H. FOOD MARKET
41-05 Union Street
Flushing, NY 11355
(Chinese delicatessen
available)

MAIN STREET FOODS, INC.
41-54 Main Street
Flushing, NY 11355

FIVE CONTINENTAL
FOODS INC.
80-19 Broadway
Elmhurst, NY 11373

W. & W. GROCERY CO., INC.
133-64 41st Avenue
Flushing, NY 11355

EAST WIND
2801 Broadway (at 108th)
New York, NY 10025

NEW FRONTIER
TRADING CORP.
2394 Broadway (between
87th and 88th Streets)
New York, NY 10024

CENTRAL ASIAN FOOD
MARKET, INC.
212 Canal Street
New York, NY 10013

CHINESE AMERICAN
TRADING CO., INC.
91 Mulberry Street
New York, NY 10013
(down a few steps)

CHINESE NATIVE
PRODUCTS, LTD.
22 Catherine Street
New York, NY 10038

GOLDEN PACIFIC
DEVELOPMENT, INC.
199-201 Centre Street
New York, NY 10013

KAM KUO FOOD
CORPORATION
7 Mott Street
New York, NY 10013
(Chinese delicatessen
available; two levels)

KAM MAN FOOD
PRODUCTS, INC.
200 Canal Street
New York, NY 10013
(Chinese delicatessen
available; two levels)

PEARL RIVER CHINESE
PRODUCT EMPORIUM INC.
13-15 Elizabeth Street
New York, NY 10013

UNITED SUPERMARKET
84 Mulberry Street
New York, NY 10013

Specialties:
MAY MAY
35 Pell Street
New York, NY 10013
(fresh and frozen
buns, dumplings and
take-home foods)

WING ON WO & CO.
26 Mott Street
New York, NY 10013
(wide and attractive
variety of Chinese
tableware and tea
sets)

OHIO

FRIENDSHIP CHINESE
FOODLAND
3415 Payne Avenue
Cleveland, OH 44114

HALL ONE CO.
326 St. Clair Avenue
Cleveland, OH 44114

SAM WAH YICK KEE CO.
2146 Rockwell Avenue
Cleveland, OH 44114

TENNESSEE

FAR EAST CO.
6914 Kingston Pike
Knoxville, TE 37919

TEXAS

ORIENTAL IMPORT AND
EXPORT COMPANY
2009 Polk Street
Houston, TX 77003

WASHINGTON, D.C.

DA HUA FOODS INC.
615-617 Eye Street NW
Washington, DC 20001

SUN KWONG HONG CO.
750 6th Street NW
Washington, DC 20001
(Chinese delicatessen
available)

TUCK CHEONG COMPANY
617 H Street NW
Washington, DC 20001

WANG'S COMPANY
800 7th Street NW
Washington, DC 20001

WASHINGTON

HOUSE OF RICE
4112 University Way NE
Seattle, WA 98105

UWAJIMAYA, INC,
6th South & South King
Seattle, WA 98104
and
688 South Center Shopping
Center
Seattle, WA 98188

VIRGINIA

CHINA GROCERY
3509 Leesburg Pike
Arlington, VA 22041

ENGLAND

CHEONG-LEEN
SUPERMARKET
Tower House
4-10 Tower Street
Cambridge Circus
London, WC 2H 9NR
ENGLAND

BAKERIES

CALIFORNIA

ACE BAKERY CAFE
1068 Stockton Street
San Francisco, CA 94108

KAY WAH PASTRY CO., INC.
1039 Stockton Street
and
1426 California Street
San Francisco, CA 94133

KOWLOON PASTRY
909 Grant Avenue
San Francisco, CA 94133
(Chinese delicatessen
available)

MAXIM'S BAKERY
1249 Stockton Street
San Francisco, CA 94133

PING YUEN BAKERY & CAFE
1066 Grant Avenue
San Francisco, CA 94133

NEW YORK

FUNG WONG BAKERY, INC.
30 Mott Street
New York, NY 10013

LUNG FONG
CHINESE BAKERY
41 Mott Street
New York, NY 10013

LUNG MOON BAKERY
83 Mulberry Street
New York, NY 10013

WINES AND SPIRITS

CALIFORNIA

METRO FOOD CO.
641 Broadway
San Francisco, CA 94133

WING SING CHONG CO.
1076 Stockton Street
San Francisco, CA 94108

WASHINGTON, D.C.

CIRCLE LIQUOR
5501 Connecticut Avenue NW
Washington, DC 20015

NEW YORK

CHAN'S LIQUOR
MARKET INC.
24 Bowery
New York, NY 10013

TAI PEI INC., RETAIL
WINE & LIQUOR
53 Mott Street
New York, NY 10013

GENERAL DISCOUNT WINES
AND LIQUORS
81-37 Broadway
Elmhurst, Queens, NY 11373

1. Almond Powder 杏仁霜

2. Bamboo Shoots, canned 清水竹筍

3. Bean Curd 豆腐

4. Bean Sprouts,
   fresh or canned 綠豆芽

5. *Bok Choy* 廣東白菜

6. "Cellophane" Noodles 粉絲

7. Chinese Cabbage (Napa) 黃芽白

8. Chinese Egg Noodles,
   fresh or dry 鷄蛋麵

9. Chinese Leeks 韮菜

10. Chinese Sausage, pork 香腸

11. Chinese Sausage,
    duck liver 鴨肝腸

12. Chinese Dried Mushrooms 香菇

13. Chrysanthemum Crystals 菊花晶

14. "Cloud Ears" 木耳

15. Fermented Black Beans 豆豉

16. Five-Spice Powder 五香粉

17. Ginger, fresh 薑薑

18. Glutinous Rice (sweet rice) 糯米

19. Ground Rice Powder,
    seasoned 五香蒸肉粉

20. Hoisin Sauce, canned 海鮮醬

21. "Instant" Noodles 即席麵

22. Oyster Sauce 蠔油醬

23. Peanuts, raw 生花生

Orient Express Chinese Shopping List

24. Preserved Cucumbers, canned 醬瓜

25. Preserved Tea Melons, canned 甜茶瓜

26. Pressed Bean Curd 豆腐干

27. Plum Sauce, canned 蘇梅醬

28. Red Bean Paste, canned 紅豆沙

29. Rice Noodles 米粉

30. Rock Sugar 冰糖

31. Sesame Seeds, black 黑芝蔴

32. Sesame Seeds, white 白芝蔴

33. Sesame Oil 香油

34. Sesame Paste 芝蔴醬

35. Shao Hsing Rice Wine 紹興酒

36. Snow Peas, fresh or frozen 雪豆

37. Soybean Milk 豆漿

38. Soy Sauce, all-purpose 醬油

39. Star Anise 八角

40. Sugar Cane and Imperatae Beverage 竹蔗茅根精

41. Szechuan Mustard Pickle 四川榨菜

42. Tea, black 紅茶

43. Tea, chrysanthemum 菊花茶

44. Tea, green 綠茶

45. Tea, jasmine 香片

46. Tea, lichee 荔枝紅茶

47. Tea, oolong 烏龍茶

48. Water Chestnuts, canned 荸薺

49. Winter Melon, fresh 冬瓜

50. Wonton Skins 餛飩皮

SHORT NOTICE

Soy Sauce Cornish Hen
Soy Sauce Chicken
  Drumsticks
Soy Sauce Chicken Wings
Soy Sauce Flank Steak
Soy Sauce "Water Lotus"
  Eggs
Soy Sauce Fresh
  Mushrooms
Soy Sauce Five-Spice Beef
Luncheon Noodles,
  Northern Style
Sweet Noodles
"Instant" Noodles
Steamed Eggplant
Boiled Spinach
Steamed Eggs

Radish Salad
Quick-Fried Romaine
  Lettuce
Corn Soup
Watercress Soup
Chinese Sausage
Steamed New Potatoes,
  Northern Style
Soy Sauce Chicken
  Gizzards
White-Cooked Chicken
(see **Store-to-Table: The
  Chinese Grocery, The
  Chinese Delicatessen** and
  The Chinese Bakery for
  additional ideas)

TEA PARTY

Choice of teas: green,
  black, chrysanthemum,
  jasmine, lichee and
  oolong
Almond "Tea"

Sugar Cane and Imperatae
  Beverage
Soybean Milk
Deep-Fried *Wontons*
Deep-Fried Sweet *Wontons*

Orient Express Menus

Baked Bean Paste Buns
Crispy Twists
Deep-Fried Sugared
   Walnuts
Baked Pork Buns

Deep-Fried Salted Peanuts
(see **Store-to-Table: The
   Chinese Grocery,
   packaged goods,** and **The
   Chinese Bakery** for
   additional ideas)

WINE PARTY

Choice of Chinese wines:
   Shao Hsing, Mou Tai,
   kaoliang, Lichee,
   Tsingtao beer or vodka;
   or Western wines: white,
   red, rosé; sherry; Scotch;
   or your favorite aperitif
Soy Sauce Five-Spice Beef
Soy Sauce Chicken
   Gizzards
Soy Sauce Hard-Boiled
   Eggs
Soy Sauce Chicken Wings
Deep-Fried Meatballs

Shrimp Chips
Deep-Fried *Wontons*
Deep-Fried Sweet *Wontons*
Baked Bean Paste Buns
Deep-Fried Sweet Walnuts
Baked Pork Buns
Chinese Sausage
Batter-Fried Potatoes
"Pearl Balls"
Steamed Buns
Soy Sauce Carrots,
   Peanuts, and Scallions
(see **Store-to Table: The
   Chinese Delicatessen** for
   additional ideas)

VEGETARIAN DISHES

Soy Sauce Mushrooms
Soy Sauce Carrots,
   Peanuts, and Scallions
Vegetable Fried Rice
Vegetarian Noodles
Steamed Eggplant
Boiled Spinach
Boiled *Bok Choy*
Quick-Fried Eggplant
Quick-Fried Bean Sprouts
Quick-Fried Romaine
   Lettuce
String Beans, Taiwan Style

Quick-Fried Snow Peas,
   Pressed Bean Curd, and
   Dried Mushrooms
Deep-Fried Sweet *Wontons*
Baked Bean Paste Buns
December 8 Festival Rice
Batter-Fried Potatoes
Deep-Fried Salted Peanuts
Deep-Fried Sweet *Wontons*
Steamed New Potatoes,
   Northern Style
(see **Salads and Pickles; The
   Chinese Grocery, canned
   vegetarian foods** for
   additional ideas)

BEGINNERS

Boiled Rice, Country Style
Boiled Spinach
Boiled *Bok Choy*
Steamed Eggs
Chinese Sausage
Pork and Mushroom Patty
Sweet "n" Sour
  Cucumbers
Corn Soup
Rice Porridge and Eggs
Plain Rice Porridge
"Instant" Noodles
Steamed Eggplant
Bean Curd Salad
Bean Sprout Salad
Radish Salad
Salted Broccoli Stems
Watercress Soup
Winter Melon Soup

Soy Sauce Flank Steak
Luncheon Noodles
Sweet Noodles
Steamed New Potatoes,
  Northern Style
Chinese Leek Omelet
Deep-Fried Meatballs
Soy Sauce Stock
Soy Sauce Cornish Hen
Soy Sauce Chicken
  Gizzards
Soy Sauce Fresh
  Mushrooms
Almond Junket
Almond "Tea"
Chrysanthemum Crystals
  Drink
Sugar Cane and Imperatae
  Beverage

FAMILY-STYLE CHINESE DINNER
(serves 4 to 6)

Choose 1 or 2 dishes from
  Column A, and 1 each
  from Columns B, C, D,
  and E

A—BEEF AND PORK
Soy Sauce Flank Steak
Soy Sauce Pork Spareribs
Soy Sauce Meatballs
Red-Cooked Beef and
  Carrots
Red-Cooked Pork and
  Potatoes
Red-Cooked Pork Shoulder
Pork and Bean Curd Balls
Pork and Mushroom Patty

Beef with Onions in Hoisin
  Sauce
Rice Powder Steamed Pork
Rice Powder Steamed
  Spareribs
(see **Store-to Table: The
  Chinese Delicatessen**)

B—VEGETABLES
Steamed Eggplant
Boiled Spinach
Boiled *Bok Choy*
Asparagus Salad
Bean Curd Salad
Bean Sprout Salad
Sweet "n" Sour Chinese
  Cabbage

Sweet "n" Sour
Cucumbers
Cucumbers with Sesame
Paste
Mixed Pickled Vegetables,
Szechuan Style
Other Pickles
Quick-Fried Romaine
Lettuce
Quick-Fried *Bok Choy*
Quick-Fried Bean Sprouts
String Beans, Taiwan Style

C—SOUP
Bean Curd Soup
Corn Soup
Duck Bone Soup
"Cellophane" Noodle
Soup
Pork and Szechuan
Mustard Pickle Soup
Winter Melon Soup
Watercress Soup
Meatball Soup

D—MISCELLANEOUS
Steamed Duck
Steamed Eggs

Steamed Flounder with
Black Beans
Chinese Leek Omelet
"Four Happinesses"
Meatball Casserole
Chinese Sausage
Soy Sauce Chicken
Gizzards
White-Cooked Chicken
Soy Sauce Hard-Boiled
Eggs
Soy Sauce Chicken
Drumsticks
Soy Sauce Chicken Wings

E—STARCHES
Boiled Rice, Country Style
Steamed Short-Grain Rice
Steamed Buns
Steamed New Potatoes,
Northern Style
Steamed Bread
Cold Noodles (plain)

OUTINGS

Soy Sauce Chicken
Drumsticks
Soy Sauce Flank Steak
Soy Sauce Five-Spice Beef
Barbecued Chicken
Drumsticks
Barbecued Pork
Soy Sauce Hard-Boiled
Eggs
Tea Leaf Eggs

Sweet "n" Sour
Cucumbers
Celery Salad
Radish Salad
Mixed Pickled Vegetables
"Instant" Noodles
Almond "Tea"
Sugar Cane and Imperatae
Beverage

BUFFET

Soy Sauce Beef Short Ribs
Soy Sauce Chicken Wings
Soy Sauce Cornish Hen
Soy Sauce Flank Steak
Soy Sauce Meatballs
Chinese Sausage Fried Rice
Cold Noodles with Sesame
   Paste
Honeyed Ham with
   Steamed Bread
Rice Powder Steamed Pork
Barbecued Chicken
   Drumsticks
Barbecued Pork

Barbecued Pork Spareribs
Sweet "n" Sour Chinese
   Cabbage
Celery Salad
Cucumbers with Sesame
   Paste
Vegetarian Noodles
Mixed Pickled Vegetables
(see **Store-to-Table: The
Chinese Grocery,
refrigerated and freezer
sections;** and **The Chinese
Delicatessen**)

HOMEMADE GIFTS

Crispy Twists
Mixed Pickled Vegetables
Deep-Fried Sugared
   Walnuts

Deep-Fried Sweet *Wontons*
Deep-Fried Salted Peanuts
Tea Leaf Eggs

BUDGET DISHES

Pork Stock
Duck Stock and Duck Fat
Duck Bone Soup
Bean Curd Soup
"Cellophane" Noodle
   Soup
"Instant" Noodles
Boiled Rice, Country Style
Steamed Short-Grain Rice
Soy Sauce "Water Lotus"
   Eggs
Soy Sauce Chicken Wings
Soy Sauce Chicken
   Gizzards
Oxtail Soup

Fried Rice and Onions in
   Duck Fat
Luncheon Noodles,
   Northern Style
Steamed Buns
Steamed Eggs
Barbecued Chicken
   Drumsticks
Bean Curd Salad
Bean Sprout Salad
Radish Salad
Chinese Leek Omelet
Almond Junket
Quick-Fried White Cabbage
   and Ham

KIDS' FAVORITES

Noodles with Meat Sauce
"Instant" Noodles
Barbecued Chicken
    Drumsticks
Barbecued Pork
Barbecued Pork Spareribs
Wontons
Wonton "Soup"
Crispy Twists
Baked Bean Paste Buns
Baked Pork Buns
Honeyed Ham, Hunan
    Style
Steamed Buns
Deep-Fried Sweet *Wontons*
Soy Sauce Meatballs

Soy Sauce Flank Steak
Soy Sauce Chicken
    Drumsticks
Cold Noodles with Sesame
    Paste
Vegetable Fried Rice
Chinese Sausage Fried Rice
"Pearl Balls"
Sweet Noodles
Corn Soup
Almond Junket
Shrimp Chips
Sugar Cane and Imperatae
    Beverage

DINNER FOR TWO

Soy Sauce Cornish Hen
"Pearl Balls"
Vegetable Fried Rice
Fried Rice and Onions in
    Duck Fat
Soy Sauce Pork Spareribs
Quick-Fried Romaine
    Lettuce
Quick-Fried *Bok Choy*
Bean Curd Salad

Sweet "n" Sour
    Cucumbers
Corn Soup
Noodles with Meat Sauce
Meatball Soup
Winter Melon Soup
(see **Store-to-Table: The
    Chinese Grocery,
    packaged goods;** and **The
    Chinese Delicatessen**)

TWO COMPLETE CHINESE BANQUETS
(serves 8 to 10)

NO. 1
Soy Sauce Five-Spice Beef
White-Cooked Chicken
Deep-Fried Sugared
    Walnuts
Special Duck (delicatessen)
Celery Salad (baby clams)
Chinese Wine

◆

Quick-Fried Snow Peas,
    Pressed Bean Curd, and
    Dried Mushrooms
Red-Cooked Pork Shoulder
    with Steamed Buns
"Cellophane" Noodles with
    Meat Sauce, Szechuan
    Style

Rice Powder Steamed
  Spareribs
Boiled *Bok Choy*
Beef with Pickled String
  Beans
Steamed Beef Buns
Crabmeat and Chinese
  Cabbage Soup
Boiled Rice, Country Style

◆

Deep-Fried Sweet *Wontons*
Fresh fruits in season
Nuts
Green tea

NO. 2
Deep-Fried Meatballs
"Cellophane" Noodle
  Salad
Soy Sauce Dried Chinese
  Mushrooms with Soy
  Sauce Eggs in Quarters
Sweet "n" Sour Chinese
  Cabbage
Chinese Wine

◆

Squab (delicatessen)
Crispy Duck with Steamed
  Buns or Mandarin
  Pancakes
Beef with Onions in Hoisin
  Sauce
Honeyed Ham Hunan
  Style with Steamed
  Bread
Steamed Flounder with
  Black Beans
Winter Melon Soup
Steamed Short-Grain Rice

◆

Baked Bean Paste Buns
Almond Junket with
  Canned Fruits
Candies (see **Store-to-Table:
  The Chinese Grocery,
  packaged goods**)
Green tea

The proper way to serve a banquet, Chinese style, is to put the first four hors d'oeuvrelike dishes on the table all at once with Chinese wine. After the toasts are over, bring out the hot foods, one at a time. Quick-Fried plates should follow those that are steamed, boiled, or otherwise prepared. However, fish will follow the other main course, and will then be followed by soup, rice and buns. Sweet things, fruit, and tea complete the feast. Throughout, guests sample only a small amount of each course and will have their own individual serving plates instead of helping themselves directly from the main serving bowl, family style. Be sure to allow plenty of time to enjoy a leisurely banquet.

If you would like to grow slender Oriental eggplant, tender cucumbers, and *bok choy* in your backyard, Chinese seeds are now widely available in many Oriental food stores. Look or ask for them in Garden World and other garden supply shops, or order them by mail. The following two companies will send catalogues:

KITAZAWA SEED
COMPANY
356 West Taylor Street
San Jose, CA 95110

TSANG AND MA
INTERNATIONAL
1556 Laurel Street
San Carlos, CA 94070

Grow Your Own

VOLUME

½ teaspoon			= approx. 2.5 milliliters
1 teaspoon	= ⅓ tablespoon	= ¹/₆ fluid ounce	= approx. 5 milliliters
1 tablespoon	= 3 teaspoons	= ½ fluid ounce	= approx. 15 milliliters
4 tablespoons	= ¼ cup	= 2 fluid ounces	= approx. 60 milliliters
16 tablespoons	= 1 cup	= 8 fluid ounces	= 236.5 milliliters
4 cups	= 1 quart	= 32 fluid ounces	= 946 milliliters

WEIGHT

1 ounce		= 28.35 grams	
8 ounces	= ½ pound	= 226.8 grams	
16 ounces	= 1 pound	= 453.6 grams	= 0.45 kilogram
2.2 pounds			= 1 kilogram

TEMPERATURE

250° F = 121° C
350° F = 177° C
400° F = 205° C

LENGTH

¼ inch = 0.63 centimeter
½ inch = 1.27 centimeters
1 inch = 2.54 centimeters

Measure for Measure

To help you budget your time, we are listing recipes according to categories of *Working Time*—preparation and cooking—and *Non-Working Time*—soaking, marinating, steeping, chilling, etc. These are only estimates, of course, as some people work quickly, others slowly. But they should give you a fairly good guide to those dishes that require only a few minutes to make, those that take about half an hour, and those that take longer. This special index will give you yet another advantage as an *Orient Express* cook.

Time Index

WORKING TIME	RECIPE	NONWORKING TIME	PAGE
	Bean Curd Salad	20 minutes salting and chilling	74
	Bean Sprout Salad	20 minutes chilling	75
	Salted Broccoli Stems	4 hours chilling	83
	Pickles: String Beans and Carrots	2 days pickling	84
	Quick-Fried Romaine Lettuce		94
	Quick-Fried *Bok Choy*		95
	Chinese Leek Omelet		97
	Beef with Pickled String Beans	10 minutes marinating, also see recipe for Pickles: String Beans and Carrots, p. 84	106
	Deep-Fried *Wontons*	see recipe for *Wontons,* p. 38	143
	Soy Sauce Hard-Boiled Eggs	6 hours steeping	159
	Crispy Duck	see recipe for Steamed Duck, p. 60	165
11 to 20 minutes	Soy Sauce Flank Steak	20 minutes steeping	6
	Soy Sauce Chicken Drumsticks	15 minutes steeping	8
	Soy Sauce Mushrooms	20 minutes soaking and 30 minutes steeping	15
	Boiled Rice, Country Style		24
	Steamed Short-Grain Rice	5 minutes resting	25
	Vegetable Fried Rice	20 minutes soaking	26
	Noodles with Meat Sauce		32
	Wonton "Soup"	see recipe for *Wontons,* p. 38	39
	Luncheon Noodles, Northern Style		40
	Steamed Buns		42
	Steamed Eggs		50
	Asparagus Salad	20 minutes chilling	73
	Sweet "n" Sour Chinese Cabbage	20 minutes salting and chilling	76
	Celery Salad	20 minutes chilling	78
	"Cellophane" Noodle Salad		78
	Pickles: White Cabbage and Red Peppers	2 days pickling	85
	Pickles: Cauliflower and Carrots	2 days pickling	85
	Quick-Fried Pork and Preserved Cucumbers	10 minutes marinating	98
	String Beans, Taiwan Style		98
	Quick-Fried White Cabbage and Ham		99
	Beef with Onions in Hoisin Sauce	10 minutes marinating	101
	Quick-Fried Broccoli		102
	Quick-Fried Snow Peas, Pressed Bean Curd, and Dried Mushrooms	20 minutes soaking	103
	Pork with Eggs and "Cloud" Ears	10 minutes soaking and marinating	104
	Quick-Fried Eggplant		105
	Deep-Fried Meatballs		107
	Batter-Fried Potatoes		108
	Bean Curd Soup	10 minutes salting	119
	Corn Soup		120
	"Cellophane" Noodle Soup	20 minutes soaking	122
	Watercress Soup	20 minutes soaking	124
	Crispy Twists		138
	Deep-Fried Sugared Walnuts	10 minutes chilling	139
	Deep-Fried Sweet *Wontons*		140
	Chinese Sausage		141
	Soy Sauce Chicken Wings	15 minutes steeping	159
	Soy Sauce Chicken Gizzards		160

WORKING TIME	RECIPE	NONWORKING TIME	PAGE
21 to 30 minutes	Soy Sauce Cornish Hen	20 minutes steeping	7
	Soy Sauce Meatballs	10 minutes steeping	12
	Soy Sauce Pork Spareribs	15 minutes steeping	13
	Plain Rice Porridge	20 minutes resting	29
	Vegetarian Noodles	20 minutes soaking	35
	Wontons		38
	Pork and Bean Curd Balls		51
	Pork and Mushroom Patty		52
	Steamed Eggplant		53
	Steamed New Potatoes, Northern Style		58
	Mixed Pickled Vegetables, Szechuan Style	2 days pickling	87
	Quick-Fried Pork with Snow Peas	20 minutes soaking and 10 minutes marinating	100
	Duck Bone Soup	see recipe for Steamed Duck, p. 60	123
	Pork and Szechuan Mustard Pickle Soup	10 minutes marinating	125
	Winter Melon Soup	20 minutes soaking	126
	Baked Bean Paste Buns		137
	Steamed Beef Buns		142
	Baked Pork Buns		143
31 to 40 minutes	Soy Sauce Duck	20 minutes steeping	10
	Soy Sauce Carrots, Peanuts, and Scallions		14
	Rice Porridge and Eggs	20 minutes resting	30
	Rice Porridge with Ground Beef or Chicken	5 minutes heating	31
	Fried Rice Noodles with Pork	20 minutes soaking and 10 minutes marinating	32
	Cold Noodles with Sesame Paste	10 minutes chilling	34
	Steamed Flounder with Black Beans	15 minutes marinating	62
	"Cellophane" Noodles with Meat Sauce, Szechuan Style		109
	Crabmeat and Chinese Cabbage Soup	20 minutes soaking	127
	Meatball Soup		128
	White-Cooked Chicken	20 minutes salting and 20 minutes steeping	158
	Barbecued Chicken Drumsticks	1 hour marinating	164
41 to 50 minutes	"Pearl Balls"	2 hours soaking	58
	"Four Happinesses" Meatball Casserole		110
	Barbecued Pork Spareribs	2 hours marinating	161
	Barbecued Pork	2 hours marinating	163
1 to 2 hours	Soy Sauce Beef Short Ribs		13
	Red-Cooked Beef and Carrots		16
	Red-Cooked Pork and Potatoes		16
	Rice Powder Steamed Pork	20 minutes soaking and marinating	56
	Steamed Duck	3 hours salting	60
	Honeyed Ham, Hunan Style		63
	December 8 Festival Rice	3 hours soaking	135
	Tea Leaf Eggs	6 hours steeping	144
2 hours and more	Soy Sauce Five-Spice Beef	1 hour steeping	10
	Red-Cooked Pork Shoulder		17
	Rice Powder Steamed Spareribs	20 minutes marinating	57
	Pork Stock		118
	Oxtail Soup		129

Index

Flank Steak, Soy Sauce, 6
Flounder, Steamed, with Black Beans, 62

G

Garden catalogues, 199
Grocery, Chinese, 149; canned and bottled products, 150; fruits, 151; names of, by state, 185-188; packaged goods, 152; pickles and preserves, 150-151; refrigerated and frozen goods, 152; vegetarian foods, 150

H

Ham. *See also* Pork
  Honeyed, Hunan Style, 63
  White Cabbage and, Quick-Fried, 99
Homemade gifts, suggestions for, 196

J

Juices, 182; Sugar Cane and Imperatae Beverage, 184
Junket, Almond, 134

L

Lu zhi. See Soy Sauce Stock

M

Measurements, 200
Meat. *See* individual names
Meatball(s)
  Casserole, "Four Happinesses," 110
  Deep-Fried, 107
  Pork and Bean Curd, 51
  Soup, 128
  Soy Sauce, 12
Menus: banquets, 197-198; beginners, 194; budget dishes, 196; buffet, 196; dinner for two, 197; family-style dinner, 194; homemade gifts, 196; kids' favorites, 197; outings, 195; short notice, 192; tea party, 192; wine party, 193; vegetarian, 193
Moon cakes, 168
Mushrooms, Soy Sauce, 15

N

Noodles
  Cellophane, with Meat Sauce, Szechuan Style, 109

  Cellophane, Salad, 78
  Cellophane, Soup, 122
  Chinese, 23
  Cold, with Sesame Paste, 34
  Instant, 36
  Luncheon, Northern Style, 40
  with Meat Sauce, 32-33
  Rice, 23; Fried, with Pork, 32
  Sweet, 41
  Vegetarian, 35

O

Oxtail Soup, 129

P

Peanuts, Salted, Deep-Fried, 144
Pearl Balls, 58
Pickles
  Cauliflower and Carrots, 85
  Mixed Pickled Vegetables, Szechuan Style, 87
  Salted Broccoli Stems, 83
  String Beans and Carrots, 84
  White Cabbage and Red Peppers, 85
Pickling Brine, 84, 87
Pork. *See also* Ham
  Barbecued, 163
  and Bean Curd Balls, 51
  with Eggs and "Cloud Ears," 104
  and Mushroom Patty, 52
  and Potatoes, Red-Cooked, 16
  and Preserved Cucumbers, Quick-Fried, 98
  Rice Powder Steamed, 56
  Shoulder, Red-Cooked, 17
  with Snow Peas, Quick-Fried, 100
  Spareribs, Barbecued, 161
  Spareribs, Rice Powder Steamed, 57
  Spareribs, Soy Sauce, 13
  Stock, 118
Pork and Szechuan Mustard Pickle Soup, 125
Potatoes, Batter-Fried, 108
Potatoes, Steamed New, Northern Style, 58

Q

Quick frying, 91, 92-93

R

Radish Salad, 82
Red-cooking. *See* Braising
Rice
  Boiled, Country Style, 24
  December 8 Festival, 135